PLATEAUS

MOVE FROM
WHERE YOU ARE
TO
WHERE YOU WANT TO BE

MIKE KAI

AUTHOR OF *THE POUND FOR POUND PRINCIPLE*

emerge
publishing
TULSA, OKLAHOMA

20 19 18 17 16   10 9 8 7 6 5 4 3 2 1

PLATEAUS — Move from Where You Are to Where You Want to Be
©2016 Mike Kai

TULSA, OKLAHOMA

Published by:
Emerge Publishing, LLC
9521B Riverside Parkway, Suite 243
Tulsa, Oklahoma 74137
Phone: 888.407.4447
www.EmergePublishing.com

Library of Congress Cataloging-in-Publication Data

ISBN: 978-1-943127-35-1 Paperback
ISBN: 978-1-943127-36-8 Digital/E-book

BISAC Category:
REL012070 Christian Life
SEL027000 Self Help/Success

Printed in the United States of America.

TABLE OF CONTENTS

DEDICATION

To Inspire Church: Thank you for growing with us in every season and through every peak and valley. You have made it a joy for Lisa and I to shepherd you.

ACKNOWLEDGEMENTS

This book is not only a project of mine but also includes the input of others of whom this book would not be possible.

First, I want to thank my wife, Lisa, for her giving me the space and encouragement to finish the manuscript. Also, to Dr. John and April Brandenburg: for burning the midnight oil in helping me to edit my thoughts without removing my voice.

In addition, I would like to thank my publisher, Christian Ophus of Emerge Publishing, for believing that there was a place for *Plateaus* in a very competitive book market.

Lastly, to the staff at Inspire Church: for being the best team for this season and journeying with us, sharing lessons with me and loving us through it all.

FOREWORD

Don't you hate being stuck? I know I do. I despise it with all my heart. Yet it seems like every day, in some area of my life, I'm always battling a plateau.

For example, I love to push myself physically. Exercise, diet, and good routines tend to produce the right results. After seeing consistent gains and progress, my physical momentum often seems to stall. The growth that once came easily doesn't come without additional effort. The progress that seemed guaranteed now feels gone, nowhere to be found.

The same could be said of my marriage to Amy. We work hard to keep our passion and communication growing. For seasons we do great, talking freely, praying consistently, and enjoying the intimacy we know God wants for us. Then one day, out of nowhere, we seem to hit a wall. Nothing visibly changes, but instead of growing closer together, things just level out. Before long, we're going through the motions, wondering where the good times went.

As a leader, I love to conquer, to win, to expand. Who doesn't? Thankfully, for extended seasons we have seen nothing but forward progress. People are growing. Systems are humming. Things are working. Until they're not. Even now as I'm writing, our economy is struggling and most people I know are hurting. Without strong financial momentum, it's way more difficult to expand. People are nervous. Leaders seem hesitant. The growth we have often enjoyed isn't as familiar to us in this season. We've hit a plateau.

As a follower of Jesus, I know I must seek Him and put Him first daily. And most days I do. Up early, I pursue the presence of God in prayer and search for His goodness in His Word. I'm led by the Spirit, sensing Him guiding me through the day. I'm growing in faith, growing in power, growing in grace. And then one day, my spiritual momentum seems to wane. Then creep. Then stall. I hit a spiritual plateau. And I hate it more than I know how to describe.

We all know what it's like to stall out in some area of our lives. Unfortunately, while we should know those challenging times will come, it seems like we're still surprised when they do. And if you're like me, instead of instinctively knowing how to press through to the next level, often times I panic, I get depressed, I become complacent, or I feel hopelessly stuck.

Thankfully, my friend Mike Kai has written an important book to help those of us who are stuck get unstuck. This is the type of book that you might read, reread, and reread again. Why? Because you cannot change what you are willing to tolerate. If you feel stuck and roll over in defeat, you will continue to be stuck.

Just the fact that you hold this book in your hand shows that you have fight in you. And if you have fight combined with the grace of God, you can move forward, you can grow, and you can see the fulfillment of God's purposes in your life, your marriage, and your calling.

I encourage you to read each page prayerfully. Ask God to show you what needs to change about what you think, what you believe, and how you behave. The only way to break out of where you are and get to where you are supposed to be is to change something. As many have said, "If you want what you've always had, do what you've always done. If you want what few have, you must do what few are willing to do."

It's time for a change.

Don't be afraid of the challenge. Don't fear what's new or different. Don't run from pain. Find comfort in being uncomfortable. Growth and comfort never coexist. If it doesn't challenge you, it won't change you. I've found in my own life and leadership that the difference between where I am and where I'm supposed to be is the pain I've been unwilling to endure. Embrace the pain. Pain always proceeds progress.

So buckle your seatbelt. Get ready for an exciting ride. The wisdom that Mike shares on each page has the potential to propel you forward. Although your breakthrough may not happen overnight, I do believe it will come. Trust the process. Trust Mike's insights. And most importantly, trust God's Spirit.

In my own life, I've found that God does more in me in the plateaus than he does on the mountaintops. If you are struggling, facing resistance, or feeling stuck, remember that God will often do something in you before he does more through you.

As Mike will show you, plateaus can be painful, but they are also necessary. God has a purpose in every season. And as you read each faith-building page of this important book, believe God is using this season to prepare you for the next. It may feel like winter now. Thankfully spring always follows winter. Let your roots grow deep. Let God's grace carry you. Let the wisdom from this book help renew your mind.

And prepare to leave this plateau to higher ground for the glory of God.

Craig Groeschel

Founding and Senior Pastor of LifeChurch.tv
New York Times Best-Selling Author

INTRODUCTION

"Something hidden. Go and find it. Go and look behind the ranges – something lost behind the ranges. Lost and waiting for you. Go!"

from The Explorer by Rudyard Kipling

As a boy, my greatest dreams launched me into becoming an explorer. Christopher Columbus, Ferdinand Magellan, Amerigo Vespucci and Marco Polo: all heroes for a fertile fifth-grade mind. Titans who sailed the seven seas, pushing beyond the line of the horizon in search of new land and never-ending adventure.

As an eight-year-old, I often hiked the mountain we call *Mauna Loa*, the second highest peak in Hawaii, rising to an elevation of 13,000 feet. The snow-capped summit seemed so close when I first started, but after a couple of hours (and soon after running out of Twinkies and hot dogs) I'd turn back. Yet my overpowering desire pushed my small-kid self on a treacherous path through tall cattails, deep gulches, and the constant threat of flashfloods. All this was beyond my mother's ever-watchful eye. She would ask, "Where've you been?"

"Oh…around!"

In 1981, I traveled to the Philippines, the ancestral homeland of my mother's family. We stayed for an entire month. While I was there, Andrew Lloyd Webber's musical, *Evita* hit Broadway, and the famous score, *"Don't Cry for Me, Argentina"* was played mercilessly in every shopping mall in Manila. It became forever ingrained in my young, impressionable frontal lobe. In a mixture of exasperation and curiosity, I said to my mother, "One day, I'm going to go to Argentina to find out why this woman keeps asking the people to stop crying for her!"

I never dreamed that that day would come, but 25 years later I did just that! I added up my airline miles and booked two tickets to Buenos Aires for a week's vacation with my wife, Lisa. But I never really found out why Evita Peron sang that phrase.

My childhood desire to enjoy new vistas and travel to places most only see on the Travel Channel has never left me. In a way, I'm still that adventurous young boy trying to get to that ever-elusive mountain peak.

I don't know who you are or what made you decide to pick up this book, but I'm glad that you did! My hope is that all of these things I share will help you, whether you are a stay-at-home mom with kids and crumbs all over the dining room table, or a pastor leading a church with great potential. You could be a business leader who's launching a new endeavor, someone striking out on their own in a food truck, either you've been inspired or perhaps you're seeking inspiration to do something you've always had a passion for. Since you've picked up this book, there's a good chance you've hit a plateau in your life. By the time you have completed reading this book, I promise that you'll be ready to tackle the next phase of your journey.

As a guide for your reading I have sectioned off the book into three parts. Part One, has to do with how we got there in the first place. Then, I'll describe the different types of plateaus and address the different descriptions of "tents" or structures we build that tend to keep us there longer than is necessary. Part Two will focus on the varying effects plateaus have on us and those who are directly benefited or affected by them. Lastly, we will conclude Part Three with how to avoid future, prolonged plateaus and then how to maximize and leverage opportunities on the journey.

Plateaus **is for anyone who has ever felt "stuck" in the same place for an extended season or period of time.** Like a sailboat languishing "in the doldrums" — a place near the equator where currents and breezes have stalled and cease to have their effect on sail and rudder — only prayers, oars, arms, and back-breaking work offer any prospect of making further progress. In everyday life, plateaus can be incredibly frustrating and discouraging, but they can also be powerfully motivating — a type of God's "recycling center" of long-unfulfilled hopes and dreams yet to be displayed in trophy cases of accomplishment.

In this book, <u>a "plateau" is defined as "any personal, professional, physical or spiritual journey that has reached a peak and leveled off." But "plateau" can also mean "a phase of stagnation."</u> Reaching the top in any field or worthwhile endeavor can prove elating and call for a pause, perhaps even for "selfies" on the summit! **However, for many reasons we'll discover in this book, 'Plateaus' can turn into resting places that have the potential to become testing and proving grounds for even greater feats.**

PART ONE

THE PROBLEM WITH PLATEAUS.
WHAT GOT YOU HERE?

Welcome. "You have arrived."

The destination does not matter. It can be that metal placard on the door of your new office, or the high five and fist bump after you've just completed a new challenge. Or, it could be that you're finally able to take that dream vacation to Hawaii that you've been saving up for – and now you've landed at Honolulu International Airport and you've been greeted by the warm, tropical breeze, the lush greenery, the intoxicating scent of a fresh flower lei, and a polite kiss on the cheek that tells you you're not in Kansas anymore.... you've arrived in Paradise.

Your plateau may be moving from a cubicle to your own office, or adding a new bar on your stripes. It's the arrival of the baby you've been praying for, or the move to a new city that has you knowing that you're in a new place. It doesn't have to be a geographical location. It can be the next stage of life; it could be a brand new season. You might've raised your children, and now have an empty nest. You might've moved from your high school bedroom, and into your new college dorm room. You might have taken a chance, rolled the dice, prayed all about it, and felt God leading you to leave that 9-to-5 to start your own restaurant.

We are all on a journey. Even if you have never moved from your hometown, it's still a journey. Your journey could be professional, or it could be spiritual. And... it is often both. Some journeys are physical challenges, like going from one size to the next smaller size, or moving from eight reps to 12 reps on the bench, increasing from two sets to four sets, adding on a 45-pound plate to that squat rack.

The amazing thing about this life and the journey we're all on is that each of us, created in the image of God, has been assigned a God-given destiny. Though we are mere human beings, we have incredible God-given potential. Our Lord has a destiny for each and every one of us to fulfill. No two people on Planet Earth are alike; no two sets of thumbprints are exactly the same. You and I are incredibly and wonderfully unique.

> Rick Warren says, *You're the only person in the world who can live your life. No one else can live your life for you, and no one else is in competition with you to complete the task Jesus gave you. ... Your uniqueness means you're the only one who can fulfill the mission that God assigned for you to complete. You Are Unique — Believe It!*
>
> **_Pastor Rick's Daily Hope_ by Rick Warren**
> **— May 21, 2014**

Because we're uniquely created and gifted by God, He has placed every one of us on our own unique journey. The big question is: Have you discovered your destination? And if you have, are you heading in the right direction?

When we think about our life journey, we often envision spreadsheets with red lines ascending vertically as it moves to the right. We think of upward mobility. Phrases like "climbing the ladder of success" and "going to the next level" have become common in our western vernacular. We strive to become all we can be, and for the Christian, we strive to become all we can be while becoming more and more like Jesus.

Some time has passed since the publication of my first book, *The Pound for Pound Principle.* Friends and colleagues have asked me from time to time, "So tell me, Mike, when are you writing your next book?" To be honest, at that time, I didn't feel that I had much new insight to offer after completing my first book. When I wrote *Pound for Pound*, the theme of the book was based on the *Parable of the Talents* in Matthew chapter 25. The insights of that principle just kept flowing out of me every time I preached, or whenever I would exhort our leaders and staff. I kept saying, "It doesn't matter how big we are, but what are we doing with what God gave us?"

I have to admit that it was easier writing that first book because it was my first effort, and it was so fresh and new. The Lord was doing something so powerful and amazing in our church that writing *Pound for Pound* seemed more biographical, and it just flowed out of our daily experience with all that God was doing at Inspire Church.

To be honest, in the first seven years, pastoring our church was a grind! Restarting a struggling church is no easy task. In fact, I think it's easier to plant and launch a brand-new, fresh team of people who want to go with you. The majority of them will have your heart, your DNA, and your expectations. Taking over a 13-year old church back in 2001 was way more difficult than I could have imagined. They had been together through five different senior pastors by the time we arrived.

My pastor asked me to pray about taking over this church on the opposite side of the island of O'ahu. They had plateaued at about 40 members, and they had never been able to grow any further. My initial reaction was "No." But after a week of prayer and seeking God with all my heart, He changed my desires to conform with His desires. Trust me, I am so glad I let go of my limited point of view and perspective, and just learned to trust Him. Lisa and I, set out with a total of 40 beautiful, faithful friends who followed us with our pastor's blessing to blend ourselves with an existing congregation. A few of the people at the existing church had been there since the founding pastor started the church. They transitioned through four more senior pastoral changes, each with a different vision and direction. They were troopers!

But they were exhausted, and they wondered what this new pastor with a "fresh vision" (they had heard that one before) was going to do to upset their world. To some extent, I had an idea of what I was supposed to do, but really, looking back, I had no clear idea. I had gleaned proven practices and principles, and I had learned as much as I could along the way, but I definitely needed more than that. I needed God to help me like never before.

We were a crockpot church in a fast-food world, filled with a few cracked pots and even some people recovering from crack. It was slow going, but as I look back, I'm glad that it was. Slowly, the Lord led me to grow in my capacity as a pastor, and He equipped me to lead this congregation. It was a long process toward my own personal growth, and leading our brand new team to grow as well. We weren't ready for the next level, and our journey, our race, seemed to be taking longer than others. This is where Jesus's example in the *Parable of the Talents*, recorded in Matthew 25, just kept resonating in me. This parable stuck to me like a little brother who won't leave his older brother's side. It nagged me, pulled at my shirt, and demanded my attention. It tagged along with me wherever I went, and wanted to hang out with me and the big boys all day long.

If songs form the background music for certain eras of our lives, I would say one particular scripture, *The Parable of the Talents,* was definitely at the top of our playlist for the first era in the life of our church. However, this doesn't mean that this parable no longer applies to our new era. Rather, *The Parable of the Talents* has become the recurring theme in the symphony God is writing at Inspire. With each new season, as God continues to do new things at Inspire, new movements are being written in the symphony that is the life of our church.

THE ERA DEFINES, THEN REFINES

Though I preached many sermons and read my Bible daily, a few good lessons stood out to me, but nothing really grabbed me like the *Parable of the Talents.* It personified the story of my life as well as the life of our church. You see, I believe we were a two-talent church with five-talent potential. Our history revealed to us that we were able to exceed our own expectations, and we thank God everyday that we get to partner with Him to add to his kingdom and build his church. We were experiencing rapid growth during the season that I wrote *Pound for Pound,* and in the years that immediately followed. I knew somewhere in the back of my mind that eventually, momentum would slow and the spikes on the growth chart would not grow as steeply as they did before. I knew that our growth would actually begin to level off, and perhaps, heaven forbid, even begin to drop toward the lower right of the graph.

About two years ago I began to prepare a sermon, but this was no ordinary message. I felt I was onto something special. In leadership venues and in our church on weekends, I kept talking about

Jesus and his inner three disciples at the top of the Mount of Transfiguration, but I never preached an entire sermon on it. In this passage, Jesus is surrounded in a cloud of God's glory, conversing with Moses and Elijah about His upcoming suffering and death on the cross.

Peter, James, and John, Jesus's closest friends, were asleep nearby. When they awoke, Peter saw Jesus in His glory talking with Moses and Elijah, and in his freshly awakened state he blurted out, **"Master, it's wonderful to be here! <u>Let's make three shelters as memorials— one for you, one for Moses, and one for Elijah</u>."**

> *About eight days later Jesus took Peter, John, and James up on a mountain to pray. And as he was praying, the appearance of his face was transformed, and his clothes became dazzling white. Suddenly, two men, Moses and Elijah, appeared and began talking with Jesus. They were glorious to see. And they were speaking about his exodus from this world, which was about to be fulfilled in Jerusalem.*
>
> *Peter and the others had fallen asleep. When they woke up, they saw Jesus' glory and the two men standing with him. As Moses and Elijah were starting to leave, Peter, not even knowing what he was saying, blurted out, <u>"Master, it's wonderful for us to be here! Let's make three shelters as memorials—one for you, one for Moses, and one for Elijah</u>." But even as he was saying this, a cloud overshadowed them, and terror gripped them as the cloud covered them.*
>
> *Then a voice from the cloud said, "This is my Son, my Chosen One. Listen to him." When the voice finished, Jesus was there alone. They didn't tell anyone at that time what they had seen.* **Luke 9:28-36 NLT**

Who can blame Peter? Jesus is conferring with Moses and Elijah, the rock stars of the Old Testament! Moses represents the law, and Elijah represents the Prophets. Jesus is the fulfillment of both the law and the prophets. The Bible tells us that they were discussing Jesus's coming exodus from this earth — which essentially is his journey to Jerusalem to suffer and die on the cross at Calvary. Scholars say that from this point forward, Christ's passion was about six months away.

"It is good to be here!" Of course it was great to be there! What a privilege and honor to be able to be in the presence these three together! This had never been seen before. Such an incredible, awe-inspiring sight would make any person want to preserve and bottle it, keep it for themselves, and stay on that mountain top forever.

It became clear to me that I probably would've blurted out the same thing if I were in Peter's shoes. "It's good to be here!"

Then Peter, rather boisterously suggests, "Let's build three shelters. Three tents. Jesus, one for you, and one each for Moses and Elijah." Sounds like a good plan to me. However, that wasn't God's plan. It wasn't in God's plan for Jesus to stay up on that mountain any longer than necessary, and that certainly applied to the disciples as well. Imagine how funny it would have been if Peter said, "Jesus, you guys can go down the mountain now. I'll just stay here and host Moses and Elijah in the Green Room." Yeah. Funny, but not funny. It wasn't God's plan for Moses and Elijah to stay on earth, and Jesus still had his most important work left to do!

The summit "high" must have been intoxicating. The view of Lebanon, Syria and Israel might've been a rare sight. Oh, and definitely, the company that surrounded the former fishermen was enough to make a future apostle "backstage all-access pass, green-room giddy!" But none of them were meant to stay there very long.

That's where it began. This passage came alive for me during that season. It was an *"Aha! Moment."* Just like the early American fortune-seekers who traveled west in search of gold, when they found the real thing after sifting through all of the fool's gold, they would lift up a real nugget of pure gold and yell, "Eureka! I found it!" (*Eureka* means "I found it" in Greek.)

In terms of vision and future momentum for my life and the life of our church, it was like discovering gold. "Eureka! I *think* I found it!"

On the weekends, I kept saying to our people, "Oh yes, it's good to be here!" A lot of people want to be here as well. I like what's happening here, but I know that there has got to be more. God has more in store for us, and it may not look like this, but according to Ephesians 3:20, I know He has more.

> *Now all glory to God, who is able, through his mighty power at work within us, to accomplish infinitely more than we might ask or think.* **Ephesians 3:20 NLT**

My friend, God has more. It may not look like it from your current point of view, but he has more for you. You may be doing great, but he has more. What does "more" look like for you? I don't know. But if you're willing to take this journey with me and give yourself two hours to read this book, I'm willing to bet that God not only knows the desires of your heart, He sees your struggle and He wants to help you get to a place in your life where you are experiencing the abundant life!

CHAPTER ONE

A WARNING SIGN OF THINGS TO COME

Something was not right. What started off as a slowly-growing dissatisfaction with the way things were around me began to gradually increase to the point of constant frustration.

I've always considered myself an over-achiever — an underdog of sorts. I grew up in a small town. At the time, its population was a little over 2,000 people, and my high school graduating class topped out at 120 students. *Honoka`a* was one of the many small towns that sprouted up around the sugarcane mills that dotted the coastlines of almost all the Hawaiian Islands. When sugar cane was Hawaii's top-grossing industry in the late 1800s to the 1970s, almost everyone came from one of these small plantation communities, unless you came from Honolulu on the island of O'ahu, the state's capital city. But sugar was becoming cheaper to grow overseas, and tourism, government and the military eventually replaced sugar to become Hawaii's main industries.

So in many ways, I was used to having these feelings of inadequacy that I was experiencing. I'm a small town kid. Raised in a small town, I lived a small town life and had a small town perspective on life. I was accustomed to being the underdog. But this was different. From a professional and ministerial standpoint, things were going great. The church was growing at a steady, incremental clip. It was just what I needed. **But even while things around me were going well, internally I was still quite unsettled.**

Looking back, I would liken my experience to a low-grade fever that hasn't quite hit the chills and body ache stage, still manageable to live with…and in my eyes, it was not intense enough to bother dealing with. That's typical. I was so deep into the forest that I couldn't see the trees. Hansel was my new name, the crumbs were gone, and I couldn't see a way out. The scary thing was that I wasn't aware that I should be looking for an escape. That's what it felt like on the inside, but on the outside, I'm sure that to those closest to me, it was highly detectable.

Prior to the epiphany of my situation, a good friend, Don Cousins, came up to me at a conference that he was leading and said, "Mike, how are things going?" One thing you need to know about me is that I'm not great at hiding my emotions or faking my expressions. I'd never be able to play poker in Las Vegas because I just don't have a good poker face. My forehead, my eyebrows, my nostrils and my breathing all would betray me. There was no use in faking it, so I just told him what I was going through. Don said, "Mike, do you think you might have a level of anxiety or depression?"

What?! I was caught off guard when he asked me that question. Yet on the other hand, I wondered to myself if what I was going through was that noticeable? I felt like saying. "Why, Yes, Don! And have you noticed that you lack a certain level of sensitivity…?"

Of course I didn't do that. He was right... on...target. Some personal things were taking their toll on me. The church was growing, and I was surely being stretched beyond anything I was used to. On top of that, I was hardly sleeping because we had just welcomed our third child into the world, and she hadn't slept through the night just yet. Yes, something was undeniably wrong.

He gave me some great advice and I began to implement it, but it just staved off what seemed to be inevitable. I did what we all do at times: I gritted my teeth, I dropped my head, and I tackled everything as if they were walls and doors...to be broken through!

I look back and chuckle now, but it's as if I could hear Sarah Palin's voice (don't ask me why) saying, *How's that workin' for ya?*" But trust me, when you're going through that many challenges, it's no fun at all.

Not a lot of people knew I felt like this. It seems that when we're going through the toughest times, we tend to hold everything closer to our vests instead of reaching out to those who might lend a hand. But that's not the way it's supposed to be. I know that for sure. I had great friends around me. I had an accountability group I met with comprised of senior pastors who all began our ministries at the same time. I'd share everything with them, and they would share their stuff, as well. It was a great help, but within a few weeks, I would unwillingly slip back to the same place all over again.

The problem was that this wasn't my old self. I didn't even recognize the person I was becoming. I am normally confident, often joyful leading people and preaching every weekend. I was slowly losing my grip.

There was a high price to pay to learn this lesson. It's funny, but when I signed up for this roller coaster, I didn't realize that whatever I did as pastor, I would always be bringing people along with me. My beautiful, precious, even-keeled wife, Lisa, was always by my side, always on the ride with me. My saving grace, Lisa.

During these especially challenging moments, I often joke with Lisa, and I'll remind her that her parents (whom I sincerely love and appreciate, by the way) originally wanted her to marry a Chinese doctor. (Did I mention that they grew to love me too?) Lisa is a first generation immigrant from China who arrived in the U.S. when she was a year old. Along with her siblings, Lisa and her parents moved to Honolulu, Hawaii. Her dad set out to claim a piece of the American Dream, and that's what he did.

Often, first generation immigrants here in Hawaii expect their children to marry within their same culture and ethnicity. I was not of the same culture. Lisa is full-blooded Chinese. She looks like one of those beautiful martial arts film heroines. Me? I'm a Heinz 57. My mother is half Filipino and half Italian. My dad is mainly of Hawaiian and Chinese ancestry, but he's also of Norwegian, Scottish, and Cherokee Indian descent. Such an interesting concoction, right?

Lisa was raised around the city of Honolulu. I was from a small town on another island. Before she gave her life to Jesus, Lisa was a non-practicing Buddhist. I was raised as a Roman Catholic. She was single and hard working. I was a single parent of a two-year-old daughter, working two jobs, plus multi-level marketing to hustle through life. We couldn't have come from two more totally different cultures. It took a while to win her parents over, even after we were married!

I chide Lisa from time to time, "If your parents could've chosen a car for you, they would have picked out an Asian mid-sized sedan. Instead, you brought home a super-charged red Ferrari. It needs a little more maintenance, but I bet you're having the ride of your life!" She agrees. But Lisa also appreciates a long, steady road rather than the frantic races through the streets of Monte Carlo. This "Ferrari" was in bad need of an overhaul. The pit-crew captain kept radioing me to come in for fresh tires. I never heard His call. "Fuel!" He said. "I've got plenty," I carelessly reasoned. The red "engine" light on the dash started flashing. ... Finally, after a few more laps, I realized that all I could manage was a slow crawl to the side of the boulevard. Someone would have to come and tow me in.

Call it what I would, or call it what you want — the lid, the capacity, the ceiling — whatever it was, I hit it! And then like a ton of bricks, it hit me back. Instantly I knew that this was not where I wanted to be. *It was **not** good to be here.*

There are all kinds of plateaus: those places or seasons of life where we feel stuck. At the time, I wasn't stuck professionally, but I was definitely stuck emotionally and spiritually. It was even affecting me physically. Plateaus have a tendency to spill over into other areas of life, and I'm very well aware of the spiritual element and how it comes into play in our everyday lives. Jesus said, "I have come that you may have life, and have life to the fullest." But before those ever-promising words were spoken, Jesus also said, "the thief comes to steal, kill and destroy."

> *"The thief comes only to steal and kill and destroy; I have come that they may have life, and have it to the full."*
>
> *John 10:10 NIV84*

> *"The thief's purpose is to steal and kill and destroy. My purpose is to give them a rich and satisfying life."*
>
> *John 10:10 NLT*

Obviously, I've gotten through that particular season of my life; otherwise, this book could not have been written yet. Like me, we've all hit plateaus in our lives, but the problem is that we try to ignore them, because we're hoping that somehow, some way, we'll get unstuck.

When we hit a plateau, we're very reluctant to admit it, perhaps because we can't easily identify or articulate it. Maybe we're in denial or we're afraid to jinx ourselves by saying it out loud, and that if we speak negatively, we might speak into existence what we definitely do not want.

Either by sheer will or by constant prayer and trusting in God, or a combination of both, our plateaus may eventually come to an end. But I believe a passive approach to will only keep one stuck longer and more vulnerable if proactive measures aren't taken. For example, if you ever swim in the ocean and experience the power of a rip current or an undertow, the inexperienced swimmer will instinctively try to swim straight for shore. Lifeguards tell us that this is the worst possible thing you could do because exhaustion will set in. As the swimmer fights against the strong outgoing current, *most are not strong enough to swim themselves out of a rip current.*

There are two different ways that you can save your own life. The first and best way to save yourself is to swim parallel to the shore until you are out of the rip current that steadily maneuvers you further and further from shore. A second way to escape the rip current is to tread water and ride the current until it loses strength further out from shore. I don't like that second option because you just don't know where that current will end and where it will take you. Some currents are so strong they can take you miles off shore, especially at the entrance to a bay. For me, riding the current out is the scariest option. I can hear the theme song of "Jaws" playing in the background. But one of the biggest deterrents that prevents us from raising our hand and signaling for help is embarrassment and we don't want to be perceived as being weak. The very best option for your survival is **not** to try to save yourself, but to signal to the lifeguard that you need help getting out of the rip tide and ride the jet-ski back to shore.

WHY PLATEAUS ARE NATURAL AND NECESSARY

One of the things I'm going to assume about you reading this book is that the title intrigued you. The cover and subtitle might have grabbed your attention, because either you're experiencing a plateau and you want to know how to move on to the next level, or you are part of an organization that is currently experiencing a plateau. It is also quite possible that you consider yourself an achiever — active, faith-filled and believing God has more in store for you. You cannot stomach mediocrity. You won't allow mediocrity to rule your life. Or, it might be that you settled for mediocrity, and you're finally fed up with it.

Perhaps you see acceptance of your plateau creeping into your thinking and you want to do something about it. You may be stuck, frustrated, and discontent. Or maybe you are the proactive type and you want to avoid getting stuck on a plateau. Whether it's a season or a force (and you'll see why later), you have no intention whatsoever of going through it.

I've come to believe that plateaus are natural and necessary. Plateaus should be a *natural* step in the progression of a life and career of someone who is approaching a level of fruitfulness and success in any area of life. ***In fact, I am of the opinion that the goal is to peak. And you cannot plateau unless you have peaked.*** Depending on the amount of talents God has given us, your peak is different from mine, the same way that mine is different than another. The goal, then, would be to peak and plateau, peak and plateau, and this dynamic progression would continue as part of the natural rhythm/ebb and flow of a vital life being lived fully and completely just as God has intended.

The key is not to plateau for too long. In some cases, there are people, businesses and organizations that rarely ever hit a plateau. That's because they have learned to anticipate changes, trends, and downturns, and they have learned to prepare for them well. Visionary leaders anticipate the peak, and while they are still on the upward climb, they begin to make necessary adjustments to go beyond it. The following two sigmoid curves illustrate what peaks, plateaus, and downturns look like.

Fig. 1

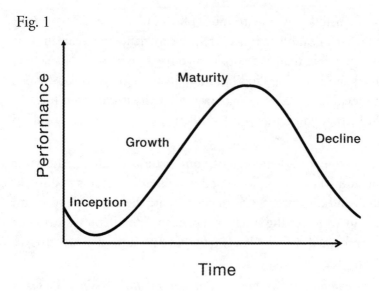

Fig. 2

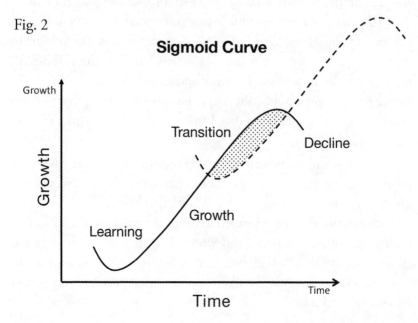

The first half of figure 1 (minus the downturn) gives us the ideal, utopian example of what we all aspire to. As I previously mentioned, it would be fantastic, and I would be ecstatic, if all areas of my life were in a steady upswing with no downturns or leveling off. But at the moment, I really can't think of any area of my personal life that follows that pattern. My life looks more like Figure 2 — peak, eventual or forecasting a plateau, avoiding of a downturn, change implementation, praying for an upswing, momentum, peak (repeat).

A plateau can be your friend, though it is most often viewed as your enemy. Through the rest of this book you will learn how to make each plateau your friend and then move on. You will also be made aware of the adversary's plan to bring you discouragement and demise in this stage of your life. For the sake of simplicity, I will most often refer to this adversary as the devil, who is real and active, and he has a multitude of workers on this earth doing his bidding. I will also refer to him as "the enemy" and "the adversary". The good news is that God is greater than the devil and has complete authority over him. Because Jesus has won the victory over sin and death, we can have that victory as well!

But while we are here on earth, the battle rages on and the struggle is real.

I believe that this book has the potential to be a great weapon to wield in the defense of your faith and to assist you in becoming all that God has called you to be. My prayer is that you will not only be inspired, you will also be equipped to fulfill all that God has planned for you. The season and the situation do not matter. You could be in the Middle-East, in a mountainside South American barrio, or on an island in the middle of the Pacific Ocean. All of us have the potential for plateaus and the potential for victory.

I believe that plateaus are a necessary reality because if you're accomplishing what you need to accomplish and becoming who you are meant to become, eventually you're going to reach a summit.

Through a well-disciplined work ethic, through lots of prayer and seeking God, and through the unmitigated providence of God's favor, you are all the more likely going to move upward. I can't determine how much higher the level will be between one plateau and the next. That's between you and God. I also can't determine for you how long it will take you to get to the next level you are trying to attain. At the end of the day, only God really knows where and when you will plateau. That's why the largest portion of this book is dedicated to exploring why plateaus can often be necessary, and helpful if handled well which launches you into a new and healthy direction.

THE HAZARDS OF CAMPING OUT ON YOUR PLATEAU

The duration of the plateau that you may currently be facing is determined by three major factors:

The *first* factor is *you and me*. Our actions, attitudes and application of lessons learned are all major contributors to how well and how soon we "swim ourselves out of it."

Second, are the *different external conditions* affecting the plateau. It could be a boss-making things difficult for you to move forward. It could be the fluctuations in the stock market, or the amount of capital that you have on hand to move forward. It could be your life choices, like the wife and mother who wants to get back to the workplace or just get out for an hour to workout, but because she's made the decision to stay at home and to raise young children, she is prevented from fulfilling her daily plans. Some plateau conditions can be beyond our control but if some of those factors are within our control require more determination and creativity to overcome.

The third and most important factor is the Lord. He will definitely have a say about how long you stay, but most of the time He doesn't intend for us to "camp out," as Peter suggested, for a prolonged period of time. God desires for us to learn the life skills and lessons we will need to use as we progress forward before He leads us on another journey of ... more climbing. I'm convinced that God is more concerned about the depth of our character than the pace of our ascent.

Everest: In 1999, author Jon Krakauer wrote *Into Thin Air,* the first-hand, personal account of his attempt to climb and summit Mt. Everest. For me, this seemed to be the perfect follow up read to *The Perfect Storm*, by Sebastian Junger. In 2015, the movie version, named *Everest* was released. Every airline that flew to Asia or Australia seemed to have this movie on their in-flight entertainment system. With so many hours on the plane and so few choices, *Everest* became the movie *du jour* for me as I partook of one of the differing varieties of rubber chicken offered to me for dinner.

The movie and the book both depict the need for base camps. Base camps are set up to replenish supplies and to get the climbers acclimated to the different environment they will experience before they climb to the next level higher. The higher they would climb, the more the climbers needed to get acclimated to the ever-decreasing supply of oxygen. As we all know, oxygen is critical to survival whether diving in the ocean or climbing a tall mountain. The higher we climb, the less oxygen is available to breathe. Oxygen is vital for one very obvious reason– breathing. Breathing of precious 0_2 is critical for brain function and mental clarity, as well as for the blood's ability to remove carbon dioxide from the entire body. Movement and actions that we normally and regularly accomplish with ease at sea level become energy-depleting endeavors at the highest elevations.

ALTITUDE SICKNESS ON MILE HIGH PLATEAUS

A few years ago, I had my first encounter with altitude sickness. It was only my second visit to South America. Remember my first vacation in Argentina? I had not been back to South America since that time.

A "chance" encounter with Robert and Karen Barriger, missionaries and pastors at *Camino de Vida* church in Lima, Peru eventually led to an invitation for me to visit them in Peru. I originally met the Barrigers while riding in the back of a shuttle van heading to the Hillsong Conference in Sydney, Australia. A former hippy, Robert got saved in the early 1970s at Hope Chapel Hermosa Beach under the ministry of Pastor Ralph Moore. When Robert and I first met, our church's name was Hope Chapel West Oahu. When he heard me mention the name of our church, he began to tell me about his spiritual journey. "What a small world!" I thought to myself. A few years after that initial meeting, Robert invited me to come to Peru to see what they do in their ministry there, and to explore the possibility that God was leading us to partner with them.

I'm so glad I took that first trip to Peru. My flight touched down in the city of Lima. I didn't know much about Peru. I'd heard some of the music before, and I'd seen some of the indigenous people playing their flutes at different places in America and around the world. It's quite beautiful, actually.

Every Friday night, "Wrestling Hawaii" was on at 8 p.m. when I was a kid. This was back in the day when there were only three channels and every kid that I knew in my hometown was glued to their television set to watch that show. One of the main characters in the wrestling world back then was called "The Missing Link." How's that for a name? And whenever the announcer would say his name over the public address system, he would say with a very low, and then a loud booming voice, "From Lima, Peru, The…Missssssinnnnnng… Link!" Prior to going to Peru, the only other facts I'd heard about Peru were about the ancient Incan city of Machu Picchu, one of South America's archaeological gems.

Robert and his son, Taylor Barriger, flew me to a town called Puna on the shores of Lake Titicaca. Lake Titicaca is one of South America's largest lakes, and it is the world's highest navigable body of water.

Prior to my flight to Peru, Robert advised me to pick up a prescription for altitude sickness pills from my doctor. Naturally, I got excited about going to a place I'd never been to before, and at an altitude I had not been at since going to the top of Mauna Kea as a child. When we landed in Puna, Robert and Taylor immediately made sure we had the best, and darkest Peruvian chocolate and coca tea, a tea made from the leaves of the coca plant — which is also used to produce recreational cocaine. They assured me that the coca tea was only a mild stimulant, that it was safe to drink, and that eating this extra-dark chocolate, and drinking this coca tea, was the best way to prevent altitude sickness.

Altitude sickness is a very real and serious medical condition. Although I had a milder version of it, I couldn't sleep at night, had some of the weirdest dreams, and lost my breath rather quickly with the slightest exertion. Although I believe I had a milder version, slurred speech, diarrhea, and pounding headaches are also common symptoms of altitude sickness. I am very thankful I didn't have the more intense version of the sickness, but Taylor did comment after the trip that he could tell that I wasn't used to that elevation. That should have come as no surprise, since I currently live at sea level at home in Hawaii. Even in the luxury and confines of what was a four-star hotel on the shore of the lake, the elevation still had its effects on me.

Before climbers ever made it all the way to the summit of Everest, they always seemed to get stuck at a critical location in the journey called "The Hillary Step." It is named after the famed explorer Sir Edmund Hillary, who with his Sherpa guide Tenzing Norgay, was the first documented human being to summit Mount Everest at the height of 29,029 feet above sea level on May 29, 1953. On the final stage before reaching the peak of Everest, just before the Hillary Step, there is a longer, very slim plateau where climbers are mercilessly beaten and buffeted by strong arctic winds, and face life-threatening hazards from avalanches and the Khumbu Icefall. Many do not make it back alive. As of 2016, there are well over 200 frozen corpses still on the mountain. But that narrow plateau isn't the main obstacle to reaching the summit. The Hillary Step is a nearly 40-foot tall vertical rock face on the southeast face of Mount Everest. Located at approximately 28,840 feet above sea level, the Hillary Step is the last real challenge before reaching the summit. This vertical ascent must be accomplished when air is at its thinnest and climbers are the most exhausted.

Who can blame those who turn back? Why risk your life to reach the peak of the world's highest mountain? The forces of nature battle against the human will as oxygen-deprived bodies and minds deteriorate at an accelerated rate because of the toll that the atmospheric conditions and thin air can take on the human body.

Yet there is an innate drive in the human spirit that is not content to merely stay on level ground. For some, the highest peaks in the world **must** be conquered, and the greatest of them all is Everest. Not everyone must go there, but if you have the insatiable drive to climb, the money to cover the substantial cost, the courage and determination to undergo extensive training and conditioning, and the willingness to physically pay the price — then why not?

Not every plateau has a Hillary step after it, where one poorly negotiated step or a sudden gust of hurricane force wind can blindside you and send you to your death. Nevertheless, frozen with fear, we hesitate to take the last steps that could take us where we've never gone before.

Some climbers just get so scared that they become paralyzed, unable to move forward. Just a while back I was talking to a friend who knew he was called to start a physical fitness business. But he never completed the application to certification. I asked him what he was waiting for? He said, "You know Mike, every time I start to pursue it, I get frozen and I can't move forward." Trust me, at that moment it took everything in not to grab his huge forearm, look at him in the eyes and to not to belt out, "Let it go, let it go!" from the Disney movie *Frozen*. Of course, as a pastor, I did my best to speak life into him and speak confidence over his future, and I did my best to motivate him to move forward into his calling.

The view from our plateaus can be just as harrowing as the Hillary Step, sending shivers of fear up and down our spine, keeping us paralyzed in a state of confusion and fear, unable to decide if we should edge forward or if we should turn back in defeat. One thing is for sure: you can't remain at the same place in life for too long. There comes a point in time when gravity begins to drag us downward. Some plateaus give way to valleys filled with trial and error, emotional highs and lows. Others take us back to a place of rest and refreshing before we try to move forward again. It never seems clear ahead of time exactly what could be waiting for us in the valleys as we descend from one plateau in search of another less treacherous path to the summit. It is seldom as bad as someone who jumps from the frying pan into the fire, making one mistake and trading it in for an even greater one. Your plateau could immediately take you on a short path to your next peak, or it could possibly descend lower before moving upward once again.

For the LORD watches over the way of the righteous,
but the way of the wicked will perish. Psalm 1:6

He makes me as surefooted as a deer,
enabling me to stand on mountain heights.
2 Samuel 22:34 and Psalm 18:33 NLT

THE LORD IS MY SHERPA, I WILL NOT DIE – – SHERPA KNOWLEDGE:

The Sherpa are an ethnic group that has lived in the high Himalayan plateaus and meadows for three centuries. Approximately 23,000 of the Sherpa people are divided into about 20 communities throughout the region. According to the Sherpa people, no peak of any of the Himalayas had ever been climbed prior to the 1950s. The Sherpa held that the Himalayas, including the summit of Everest, were the habitation of a pantheon of their gods.

At the beginning of the 20th century, British explorers first hired these traditional potato farmers to serve as porters for their expeditions. In 1953, Sir Edmund Hillary hired a Sherpa, Tenzing Norgay, as both his porter and guide, as he attempted to be the first man to reach the summit of Mount Everest. Upon his success, the extraordinary skill and abilities of the Sherpa became known worldwide. The Sherpa men quickly became experts in western mountaineering techniques, and rather quickly, serving as porters and mountain guides to the growing number of people who attempted to climb Everest and other Himalayan peaks became the primary source of income for many Sherpa families.

Sherpas are renowned in the international climbing and mountaineering community for their hardiness, expertise, and experience at very high altitudes, so much so that the word "sherpa" has come to be used to refer to any expert mountaineering guide. It has been speculated that a part of the Sherpas' climbing ability is the result of genetic adaptation over centuries of living at high altitudes. Some of these adaptations include unique hemoglobin-binding capacity and doubled nitric oxide production. Sherpas are highly regarded as elite mountaineers, among the best in the world, but it is their expertise in their local region that has made them so valuable to those who attempt to conquer Mount Everest. Dwelling in the Himalayan region for centuries, they serve as expert guides to the extreme altitude peaks and passes in this region. They know the location of every pass, every hazardous rock-fall, icefall and crevasse, and they are able to identify where the danger of avalanche is greatest. Sherpas understand the local weather conditions, and they are able to read with great accuracy the signs of storms coming their way. Serving as porters as well as guides, they skillfully pre-position supplies for the climbers, then guide them from camp to camp.

Each year, sherpas establish and fix a specific route up Mt. Everest, toiling long hours on the mountain. The stakes are high. They very deliberately establish and prepare a safe route over the difficult terrain for hundreds of climbers and the Sherpas' guided clients who will attempt to summit Everest that year. They pre-position and maintain the climbing ropes on the rock faces, install ladder bridges across gaping ice crevasses, and groom the trails at the beginning of each climbing season. Climbers place their lives and safety in the care of these exceptional guides.

If life is lost on the mountain, it is often the Sherpas who have died while serving as porters for the climbers. They are the ones who carry all of the tents, food, fuel, ropes, technical equipment, and most importantly, the oxygen supply to forward camps, crossing the deadly Khumbu Icefall multiple times before they lead the way up the most hazardous portions of the mountain. In 2014, thirteen Sherpas were killed in a single day when a deadly avalanche swept across the Khumbu Icefall as they ferried loads for the climbers to the next camp.

(Information gathered from *Sherpa people: Mountaineering, on Wikipedia.com;* and from *Sherpas: The invisible Men of Everest; Mount Everest's Deadliest Day Puts Focus on Sherpas; and Sherpas Dead in Avalanche, National Geographic.com)*

The Climber's Psalm
(Adapted from Psalm 23)

The LORD is my Sherpa;
  I will not fall to my death.
He carries my load to well-stocked camps;
  He bears heavy burdens that I could not bear.
He leads me up the mountain with skill.
  He guides me along right paths,
  Having set the ropes and bridges in place.
Even when I tread the narrowest ridges,

I will not be afraid, for you are near,
　　Close at hand to guide my way.
Your skill and your wisdom
　　protect and comfort me.
You acclimate me to thin air
　　on the highest plateaus.
You bandage my wounds
　　And treat me with care.
Surely the majesty of the summit will stay with me
　　all the days of my life,
And when I am old,
　　My Sherpa will guide me
　　safely to my eternal home.

Just as the Sherpa guides the climber through dangerous passes and ice-falls on the side of the mountain, so the Lord is our expert guide as we face the pitfalls of life's plateaus. He knows when we need to rest and acclimate before climbing higher. Long before we reach our plateau, He prepares the path ahead of each season of our lives. He pre-positions spiritual gifts and passions to prepare us for what lies ahead. He shares his skills and wisdom with us, so that we can reach the next summit without fear or injury. He walks with us all along the way, waiting to celebrate with us when we reach the summit. He has borne the cost of our safety with His own life on the cross. He leads and equips us to achieve our peak potential in His Kingdom for His eternal glory, then guides us safely to our eternal home.

THE BONEYARD OF DREAMS AND POTENTIAL

Plateaus can be holding patterns. Airport control towers often direct pilots to fly in a holding pattern because they need the time to clear the runways of planes taking off, or other planes are flying in for landings at the same time. At other times, the weather has created unsafe conditions for landing and they will need to circle until the weather clears. Pilots are often told to fly in large circles at different altitudes, or in some rare cases, they are instructed to land at a nearby airport, refuel, then return for a landing.

Plateaus can be staging grounds — places where we wait for further instruction. Till then, we "hurry up and wait." Sadly, some geographical plateaus can become the boneyards for retired prop-planes and older jet aircraft that are unused and unwanted. Former flying fortresses and other magnificent aircraft that have been worn out from overuse, have outlived their effectiveness, and are no longer safe to fly after too many miles have been logged; they are lined up in rows like gravestones in a military cemetery. Planes are retired to the boneyard when innovation and technology have rendered them obsolete, and replacement parts are no longer available to repair them.

These boneyards are stark reminders of a life in which someone's original dreams and potential had been realized, but they never had the chance to be repurposed for a new season of usefulness. They remind me of lives that have been lived out in quiet desperation when the holding patterns never launched them into new stratospheres. When I see these boneyards, I think of all the amazing adventures these once proud aircraft had embarked upon: carrying young servicemen and servicewomen to distant lands, flying weary travelers venturing to exotic vacation locations, ferrying businessmen and government officials from coast to coast and around the world, and waging daring battles in the sky and on the ground. Families were reunited on these metal tubes, others were carried to their final resting place. Heroes flew missions in them, but now these once vital, useful planes rest in a massive boneyard at Davis-Monthan Air Force Base in Tucson, Arizona where they are scavenged for parts for other aging aircraft.

There are three factors that determine how long we stay on the plateau. **The first** determining factor has to do with the person in

27

the mirror: self-perceptions and certain attitudes, apprehensions and mentalities can all be ingrained deeply in our minds, learned behaviors etched in our consciousness by our experiences, as well as the influence of those around us. I've come across many people who for one reason or another, have been unable to grow beyond their current life situation and have not been able to effectively move on to the next stage of their life.

In order to gain comfort, they latch on to philosophies and schools of thought that comfort them. In other words, they found something to justify their reason for not advancing, and they can become critical and resentful toward those who are moving forward. Or they can try to lure others around them to join them in the doldrums, so they no longer feel pressured to move beyond the status quo. These instincts to seek out mental and emotional retreats need to be abandoned if they are ever going to move beyond their plateau.

Secondly, there are situations in life that are beyond our control that can force us into a stalemate or a holding pattern. In the introduction to this book, I mentioned the doldrums, places where people grow impatient as they wait for the winds of life to shift and pick up or they paddle endlessly just to gain some forward progress and positive momentum. This could include the child that gets sick and prevents you from going back to college to get that long-postponed college degree. It could be the corporate downsizing that led to massive lay-offs and the end of your steady lifelong career. It could be the departure of your unfaithful spouse or the death of a loved one that caused your setback. The list of situations that could cause us to stall on a plateau is endless.

How we cope with these life situations that impede our progress has mostly to do with our general perception or outlook on life. Our basic disposition and perspective on life come from two different sources, nature and nurture. Some of these aspects of our personality are written in our DNA as an emotional bent or disposition with us from birth. One person may naturally be content or easy-going.

Another person may be predisposed to melancholy or approach all of life with a certain intensity. Are you an optimistic person that sees the glass half-full, or do you tend to lean toward pessimism and see the glass as half empty? The other source of our outlook and perception of reality comes from the way we were raised or nurtured by our parents and family, the experiences of our past, and the people we work and associate with. If these influences have tended to be positive, our outlook on our life situation will be positive and optimistic. If these influences have tended to be negative, our outlook on our life situation will tend to be negative and fatalistic, though some people manage to have a great outlook even though their life has been rough. They have chosen to be overcomers.

The third and most important factor is the Lord. The One who overcame death and the grave can help us to overcome the greatest obstacles and challenges in life. Because Christ is the Great Overcomer, we can become overcomers too. Our natural situation may be bleak and offer few opportunities, but we serve a supernatural God who can create opportunities out of nothing, just as He created the universe out of nothing. With God, plateaus are always the land of opportunity and hope — a place of rest, re-tooling, re-outfitting with supplies, a place of character growth, learning the lessons and life skills we'll need to employ as we enter the next stage of our journey. Paul states in

Romans 8:28-30 NIV84,

> And we know that **in all things God works for the good of those who love him,** who have been called according to his purpose. For those God foreknew he also **predestined to be conformed to the likeness of his Son**, that he might be the firstborn among many brothers. And those he predestined, he also called; those he called, he also justified; those he justified, he also glorified.

God will always turn our life plateaus to his purpose. He will use our obstacles and challenges to make us more and more like Christ. He does not care how long we spend on the plateau as long as He can accomplish His purposes while we are there. Ultimately, His desire for us is to shine like Jesus did on the Mount of Transfiguration. So we cannot stay camped on the plateau indefinitely.

In my life, I have plateaued too many times to count but my season on the emotional plateau was not a good place to be. Unlike Peter, I had discovered (referring back to pg. 16) that it was "not good to be here." But looking back I can say now that it was *good* for me. I would never want to go back there again but the lessons I learned there have proven to be invaluable and I believe they will help you as well. I believe we are either headed for a plateau, are currently stuck on one, or are coming out of that season. But in hindsight, I've discovered that as we move from glory-to-glory and peak-to-peak, there are plateau-hazards out of our view. As the saying goes, *knowledge is power.* And God has equipped and empowered you and I to recognize the challenges to face the new battles ahead.

CHAPTER TWO

FIVE MAJOR TYPES
OF PLATEAUS

Over the years, I've come to recognize that there are five major types of plateaus that you may experience in everyday life: The Never-Saw-It-Coming Plateau, The Writing-On-The-Wall Plateau, The Settled-For Plateau, The King-Of-The-Hill Plateau, and The Hit-My-Capacity Plateau. Each has its own distinct characteristics and pitfalls, but none of them have to be permanent. I'm convinced that seventy percent of the problem is remedied simply by diagnosing what stage we are in. Once we know where our ceiling is and what our sticking points are, then we can get moving toward an action plan toward health and progress.

THE NEVER-SAW-IT-COMING PLATEAU:

The **Never-Saw-It-Coming Plateau** is exactly what it sounds like. Like the proverbial frog in the pot who never notices the water temperature slowly rising to the boiling point until he's thoroughly cooked, you are up to your chin in life challenges. As time slowly passes, you fail to notice the subtle changes in your life situation, the slow downward trend, until your life is cooked. Most of the time, we are caught unaware, blinded by busyness or our preoccupation with the details of life. This may be the result of a lack of diligent self-assessment, or you may have abdicated the responsibility for your life choices to someone else, or even a group of people, and when you finally check in on the status of your life, the news hits you and you are shocked to discover that you're stranded on a plateau with no exit in sight.

A good example of someone stuck on the **Never-Saw-It-Coming Plateau** is Eli, who was the High Priest of Yahweh at the end of the period of the Judges. (1 Samuel 2:11-4:22)

For years, Eli had negligently looked the other way as his sons, Hophni and Phinehas, greedily ignored God's commandments regarding the proper handling of the sacrifices and offerings brought to His altar at Shiloh. When Eli was warned by a man of God (and later confirmed by Samuel) that God was going to bring judgment upon the house of Eli, that Hophni and Phinehas would both die on the same day, and that no member of his household would reach the age required to serve as priests at God's ever again, he did not tear his clothes in lamentation and repentance, but just simply replied, "It is the Lord; let Him do what seems good to Him." (1 Samuel 3:18)

And when a runner from the battlefield reported that Israel had been defeated, that Hophni and Phinehas had been killed on the battlefield, and that the Ark of the Covenant had been captured and taken as war-spoils by the Philistines, Eli fell over backward in a dead faint, broke his neck and died. In truth, Eli had been stuck on a plateau of neglect for years, and he **Never-Saw-It-Coming.**

THE WRITING-ON-THE-WALL PLATEAU:

The **Writing-On-The-Wall Plateau** is taken from the biblical account of Belshazzar's fateful party. In the fifth chapter of the Book of Daniel, King Belshazzar of Babylon foolishly decided to throw a banquet for a thousand of his nobles that he served sacrilegiously in the sacred vessels looted from the Temple of Yahweh in Jerusalem. There's nothing wrong with throwing a party as long as you don't blaspheme and insult God while doing so. While Belshazzar and his nobles were partying and getting drunk, the armies of Darius the Mede were massing outside the walls of Babylon, waiting for the prime opportunity to enter the city for an unexpected regime change. Midway through the festivities, the finger of God began to inscribe a cryptic message on the walls of the hall for all to see: *Mene, mene, tekel, upharsin.* The phrase was interpreted by the prophet Daniel to mean, "Your days have been numbered and double-checked twice. You have been weighed in the balances and have not measured up. So your kingdom will be divided between the Medes and the Persians." Later that night, King Belshazzar was slain by Darius's invading army.

The primary component to the **Writing on the Wall Plateau** is hubris, or arrogant pride. If **"Never-Saw-It-Coming"** is the appetizer, or the side order, then **"Writing-On-The-Wall"** is the main dish! There's nothing like pride and hubris to go along with abdication.

The king's arrogance ultimately led to his monumental moment of failure — bringing out the articles of gold and silver of the Temple in Jerusalem to party with. Sacrilege! To have the audacity to challenge God, mock Him and test Him, and blaspheming Yahweh and pridefully claim victory over Him, is just asking for the wrath of God. The shameless arrogance and ostentation that was happening on the inside of Belshazzar's hall that night and the strategic maneuvering of Darius and his army on the outside of Babylon, plugging up the city's waterways to have his armies march into the city through the empty water channel was just the apex of over ten years of bad choices by the leaders of Babylon. It was King Nabonidus's ten-year absence and abdication of his royal responsibilities and duties to his son Belshazzar as Regent (he was only acting as King in his Father's absence) and Belshazzar's youthful arrogance that led to years of terrible policies and practices during his tenure as Regent that set the scene for what was going to transpire later that night. God was not the only one angered by the selfish ostentation and disregard for the basic duties and responsibilities of King Nabonidus and his Regent Belshazzar; the Babylonian people were so angry and frustrated that they actually greeted Darius and the army of King Cyrus of the Medes and Persians as deliverers from the tyranny they had endured for the previous ten years. Babylon fell without a fight. Nabonidus and Belshazzar **"never saw it coming"** even though the **"writing was on the wall"** occurred well before the hand of God inscribed it in plaster.

In other words, the **Writing-On-The-Wall Plateau** doesn't happen over night. Just as a church or business or an individual life are almost never overnight successes, so too, their demise and fall do not happen overnight. A plateau can actually be an act of mercy, warning you of troubles that lie ahead. In some cases, this can be a warning sign from the Lord; *"Get your act together. I'm here waiting to help you. Partner with me to get back on track!"*

Can I just share with you what is always in the back of my mind? To be honest, I never want to find myself in this situation. A plateau can be a staging ground for the next season of growth, or it can be the warning signal of a downturn ahead. If we do not steward a plateau well by making the necessary changes and preparations, then the plateau and accompanying loss of momentum will eventually lead to inevitable decline. It depends on what we do when the warning signal lights up in our brains. The warning light can set us back on course to growth and increase, but if we're riding the wave of momentum and feeling like the "King of the Hill," if things are going our way and we presume the sweet spot is going to last forever, it can be even more difficult to notice the warning lights.

There's nothing like a good, old-fashioned plateau to get our attention. But the **Writing on the Wall Plateau** actually means that there are signs along the way that we have either missed or ignored. We've been given ample opportunity to make the changes that need to be made. If it's your marriage, it may be your spouse who is voicing their concerns, or they may be continually sad, angry or depressed. If it's your family, it may be a child that's crying out for attention the only way he or she can express that something is wrong. If it's your business or church, it may be foreboding statistics or employees who are expressing concerns that you need to hear. Hopefully, you and I are heeding the warning signs and listening to what is being said, and we're also noticing what's not being said.

That's why it's so important to look at the mirror and really see your own reflection. Is there accountability in your life? Are there people who love and respect you who are willing to help you catch those blind spots? We may have enough pockets of those loving people who will say what we need to hear, but they can only be of help if we're willing to make ourselves vulnerable. We can have all the accountability in the world, but if we prefer not to be totally transparent, open and honest with them, then we are only keeping up appearances, and our pride will cause us to waste this excellent source of truth.

> *And you will know the truth, and the truth will set you free."* **John 8:32 NLT**

If our arrogance causes us to ignore the truth, then we'll remain captive to whatever life plateau we find ourselves stuck in.

We all know stories about situations where great growth and increase were followed by a quick and spectacular collapse. In Jim

Collins's book, *How The Mighty Fall*, one of the biggest lessons I took from that book is what's called "the hubris of leadership." This happens when we, as leaders, do whatever we want to do just because we feel that we can. For example, if a business is great, even excellent at doing one specific thing well, and they experience success or even acclaim, they may foolishly begin to over-diversify and experiment with other opportunities that take them away from their primary focus. A lot of resources may be diverted into the implementation and expansion of this new area of interest. Before they know it, the main thing that got their business to thrive in the first place is neglected and begins to decline. This is a prime example of what happens when we allow our prideful egos to lead us to venture into areas that are outside our area of strength and excellence and divert our focus from that main thing.

That's why it's important to pay attention to the warning signs while you are still experiencing growth and increase, even before you reach the plateau. I can tell you from personal experience that there have been many times that I have been tempted to open a store, invest more in real estate, create a new brand. I know that God has given me some gifts and talents that He has used well in the body of Christ and has led to a season of great fruitfulness. That primary gift finds its sweet spot when I serve as the pastor my church. But there is a difference between a gift and a grace. Every single one of us is gifted by God to do something, and these gifts can be applied to several types of situations. A grace is a unique mix of gifts and calling that God gives you to do that **one thing** that only you can do. I am gifted to preach and teach the Bible in the life of our church, but in this season of my life, my primary calling is not to be an itinerant preacher like some of the great preachers have been gifted to be. We both use our preaching and teaching gifts, but I am gifted to pastor a church but I also believed that I am graced be a leader and bridge-builder in my denomination, my community, my state, and my country. Just as others are not graced to do what I do, at this time, neither am I graced to do what they do. Make sense?

THE SETTLED-FOR PLATEAU:

I know that a lot of us preachers will have some explaining to do when we meet Peter at the pearly gates. We have all used him in our exhortations and illustrations to our advantage. His foot-in-mouth syndrome and his impetuous behavior have, for almost 2000 years, given us some of the most memorable, and at times, the most humorous sermon material that a preacher could ever ask for! Having said that, allow me to take a little bit of creative margin here to give tribute to this great apostle — "It's wonderful to be here!"

At some point in your life and career, you might have thought to yourself, "Ah, this is good. In fact, this is good enough." That phrase is the essence of what "settling for" means.

In my previous book, *The Pound for Pound Principle*, I've addressed the difference between contentment and complacency. There's nothing inherently wrong with being content. In fact, Paul teaches us that contentment is one of the most important Christian virtues, one that he consistently modeled for every believer, especially the leaders of the church.

> *Not that I was ever in need, for I have learned how to be* ***content*** *with whatever I have.   Philippians 4:11 NLT*
>
> *So if we have enough food and clothing, let us be* ***content****.*
>
> *1 Timothy 6:8 NLT*

Who wants to live their life always striving but never feeling satisfied, always looking for more without enjoying life along the way? No matter who you are, it's a tired way to live.
Proverbs and Ecclesiastes often speak about the folly of discontent.

*Everything is **wearisome** beyond description. No matter how much we see, we are **never satisfied**. No matter how much we hear, we are **not content**. Ecclesiastes 1:8 NLT*

*What does a man get for all the toil and **anxious striving** with which he labors under the sun? Ecclesiastes. 2:22*

The tenth commandment prohibits covetousness, the sin of never being content, always wanting what someone else has that you don't have.

*"**You must not covet** your neighbor's house. You must not **covet** your neighbor's wife, male or female servant, ox or donkey, or anything else that belongs to your neighbor."*

Exodus 20:17

Jesus also taught about the inherent danger in our natural predisposition to selfishness and discontent.

And he told them this parable: "The ground of a certain rich man produced a good crop. 17 He thought to himself, 'What shall I do? I have no place to store my crops.'

18 "Then he said, 'This is what I'll do. I will tear down my barns and build bigger ones, and there I will store all my grain and my goods. 19 And I'll say to myself, "You have plenty of good things laid up for many years. Take life easy; eat, drink and be merry."'

20 "But God said to him, 'You fool! This very night your life will be demanded from you. Then who will get what you have prepared for yourself?'

21 "This is how it will be with anyone who stores up things for himself but is not rich toward God."

22 Then Jesus said to his disciples: "Therefore I tell you, do not worry about your life, what you will eat; or about your

*body, what you will wear. 23 Life is more than food, and
the body more than clothes.*   *Luke 12:16-23*

On the positive side, Paul sums up the value of righteous contentment this way:

*But godliness with **contentment** is great gain.*   *1 Tim. 6:6*

But there is a big difference between being content and being complacent, between being self-satisfied and being unaware of possible dangers that lie in resting upon your success and failing to do all that is required of you by God. If you do a Bible search on the word "complacent," it is almost always in a negative light, usually as the grounds for God's impending judgment. Here are a few examples:

*At that time, I will search Jerusalem with lamps and punish
those who are **complacent**, who are like wine left on its
dregs, who think, 'The LORD will do nothing, either good
or bad.'*   *Zephaniah 1:12 NLT*

*Woe to you who are **complacent** in Zion, and to you who
feel secure on Mount Samaria, you notable men of the fore-
most nation, to whom the people of Israel come!*

Amos 6:1 NLT

*Within a year and a few days,
You will be troubled, O **complacent** daughters;
For the vintage is ended,
And the fruit gathering will not come. Isaiah 32:10 NASB*

*At that time, I will send swift messengers in ships
    to terrify the **complacent** Ethiopians.
Great panic will come upon them
    on that day of Egypt's certain destruction.
Watch for it! It is sure to come!*   *Ezekiel 30:9 NLT*

Scripture is clear about how the Lord feels about complacency. Clearly God is displeased, even angered, by those who **settle for "good enough,"** rather than doing all that God requires as well as striving for the excellence of God's best. The same can be said of complacency's twin siblings, laziness and sloth, and their cousin gluttony.

While we can see that complacency is a major element of the **Settled-For Plateau,** its counter part, contentment, can be part of the cure. Contentment is the reward for a life well-lived in the present. I call it a reward because it's the wonderful feeling of satisfaction you get when you have done a good job. It's also the reward that accompanies doing the right things the right way, even when you are not experiencing any noticeable advancement. I have more to share on contentment later in this book.

When satisfaction gives way to slumber, you've begun the slippery slide from contentment to complacency. You've camped too long in your contentment, and rested too long on your laurels, and suddenly you've found yourself dwelling on the **Settled-For Plateau.** Complacency opens you up to all kinds of other pitfalls and hazards such as laziness, sloppy habits, and cynical thinking. The problem with this plateau is that you've completely lost your vision and your forward momentum, and the extra effort required to begin moving forward again may not feel as though it's worth the effort. Phrases like *"This is good enough,"* become a standard part of your vernacular that begins to influence and affect the attitude of those around you as well. At this point, there may be a tendency for those who want to do more and become more for God to become increasingly critical. People start questioning your motives and become suspicious of your actions in a way that is neither helpful nor productive. If you recognize that you're dwelling on the **Settled-For-Plateau,** you've already been there for too long and you've gotten too comfortable. Get off of that plateau as soon as you can for your sake and the sake of those who have been waiting to move on with you. Begin moving forward again with God, and inspire us all!

THE KING-OF-THE-HILL PLATEAU

The **King-Of-The-Hill Plateau** could be brought on by a position that you hold, a title that you have received, or just by the sense that you have accomplished all there is to accomplish in life. If we're not careful, we can soon turn into little Napoleons and become tyrannical dictators of our own petty hilltop kingdoms because our success has gone to our heads.

Both the **Writing-On-The-Wall Plateau** and the **King-Of-The-Hill Plateau** share the characteristic of arrogant pride. Though similar to the **Writing-On-The-Wall Plateau**, the **King-Of-The-Hill Plateau** has unique features that set it apart. The type of pride that leads to the **Writing-On-The-Wall Plateau** is an impetuous, heady pride that is so intoxicated by power and position that it fails to notice, or chooses to ignore, the signposts warning of the danger that lies ahead. The kind of pride that leads to the **King-Of-The-Hill Plateau** is the pride of the over-achiever who has it all, and has accomplished it all. This person is at the height of his career and at the top of his game; he's the uncontested leader in his part of the world or in his particular market or industry (or at least he is in his own eyes). This person thinks he can do whatever he wants to do, buy whatever he desires to buy, and jet to wherever he wants to go, without any regard for what God requires. It's a dangerous place to be.

The King of the Hill, if you remember from your childhood, is a game in which the strongest and cleverest person usually dominates over all. The other children try to climb to the summit of the hill from all different directions. The object is to push all of the other children down so that the best player can stand alone at the top as King of the Hill. In the game of life, the King of the Hill is the person who has stepped over or on top of everyone else in order to achieve the pinnacle of their success.

41

Pride goes before destruction,
and haughtiness before a fall. Proverbs 16:18

Ironically, the best biblical example of **the King-Of-The-Hill Plateau** is King Solomon, the author of Proverbs 16:8.

Few individuals in all of history have ever reached the pinnacle of success that was reached by King Solomon. He was the richest man alive. He controlled the two of the most strategic and lucrative trade routes in the world. He excelled in wisdom and knowledge above all others in his generation, composed over 3,000 proverbs, and also wrote three books of the Bible. He ruled the largest empire in the Middle East of his day, and his entire kingdom enjoyed unprecedented peace. He was fully entrenched on **the King-Of-The-Hill Plateau.**

Yet, all of that wasn't enough to satisfy Solomon. Once he had reached the pinnacle of success, Solomon tried to secure his place as **King-Of-The-Hill** for his descendants. He entered into countless treaties with every known kingdom and tribe to secure his borders and extend his economic reach, and amassed over 700 wives and 300 concubines (or gift-wives) as security for those agreements. He built innumerable monumental buildings and fortresses throughout his land to ensure his memory would last for millennia, and taxed his own people to pay for them because the enormous riches collected as customs and tariffs on the King's Highway and the Way of the Sea weren't enough to finance his prodigious building projects. Solomon conscripted his own citizens as craftsmen and laborers because the workers supplied by his client kingdoms weren't enough to complete the necessary work. Worse yet, he gave in to his most significant wives' demands for a place to worship their native gods, so he built the temples for them to worship their idol gods. Solomon tried everything he could to secure his place as **King-Of-The-Hill** so he could pass everything on to his son, Rehoboam and the future kings of Israel but this led to a massive revolt when Solomon died that divided his kingdom and left his descendants to rule a small remnant state, roughly one-sixth of the size of his former empire.

But what if we chose to work the game another way? What if the King of the Hill actually helped everyone else get to the top of the hill with them? What if the King of the Hill understood that in real life all ships rise on the same tide? So instead of dominating the game and throwing everyone else off of their attempt to get to the top of the hill, what would happen if we all got off of our high horses and helped everyone else to get where we already are? That would be revolutionary! Then **the King-Of-The-Hill Plateau** would become a gateway for everyone to achieve their full potential. If Solomon had played the game by these new rules, the course of history may have played out very differently, and Israel may have never been divided.

THE HIT-MY-CAPACITY PLATEAU:

The **Hit-My-Capacity Plateau** is like the "I've fallen and I can't get up" commercial on daytime television. The point is that there used to be forward movement and action in your life, but at some point you stumbled to keep up, you lost your balance and fell, or someone else knocked you down, and you've come up against an obstacle that you do not have what it takes to get past. Now it seems impossible for you to go any further or higher, and you have given up trying. John Maxwell calls this "The Law of the Lid."

> I often open my leadership conferences by explaining the Law of the Lid because it helps people understand the value of leadership. If you can get a handle on this law, you will see the incredible impact of leadership on every aspect of life. So here it is: leadership ability is the lid that determines a person's level of effectiveness. The lower an individual's ability to lead, the lower the lid on his potential. The higher the individual's ability to

lead, the higher the lid on his potential. To give you an example, if your leadership rates an 8, then your effectiveness can never be greater than a 7. If your leadership is only a 4, then your effectiveness will be no higher than a 3. Your leadership ability—for better or for worse—always determines your effectiveness and the potential impact of your organization. http://www.johnmaxwell. com/blog/the-law-of-the-lid

You have too much on your plate, too many balls in the air, and you've reached the limit to what you can do. You are at capacity. What often happens in real life is that critical life situations interrupt your focus and unexpectedly demand your attention while you're trying to focus on doing your best at work or in ministry. A family problem arises, something happens to your health or the health of a loved one, there's a death in the family, or your house burns down.... When added on top of your already demanding job and normal life responsibilities, there's only so much that you can take before you can't take any more. You've reached overcapacity.

But the **Hit-My-Capacity Plateau** does not have to last forever. Your capacity can increase. In fact, a plateau is a great place to work on increasing your capacity.

Sometimes God graciously puts us on the **Hit-My-Capacity Plateau** so we can rest and be healed and refreshed. Yes, this is one time that we can blame it on Him! But don't get into the habit of doing this all the time. Sometimes this is God's way of slowing His child down a bit. After your capacity has been reached, you begin to settle into a new normal on the **Hit-My-Capacity Plateau.** If you are wise, after you've rested for a brief season, you will begin to re-examine who you are, and what you are called and gifted to do in life. This can be a great time of introspection. You would also be wise to ask your friends and family for their encouragement and wise counsel regarding your calling and life purpose.

At its best, the **Hit-My-Capacity Plateau** can be a time of recalibration and rest. I like to use this time to evaluate everything around me: my health, my personal habits, my diet (is what I'm eating helping me or hurting me?), my routine, my relationships, ... I even see a counselor two to three times a year. (Yes, I really do go to counseling.) When I see this counselor, I open up, and I share my concerns, insecurities, anxieties, whatever I want to share... but I don't wait until after I've hit the wall, or I've crashed up against an impenetrable ceiling. I get regular counseling and wise counsel as a preventative measure to keep increasing my capacity for what lies ahead.

I try to be pro-active by keeping up my mental health and physical fitness with nutritional supplements, a healthy diet, good rest, and regular exercise. Instead of getting the diagnosis and taking medication for it, why not try to avoid getting sick, worn out, and exhausted in the first place?

The most important step I take to stay on course with my life is to spend time daily with God. I listen to His instruction in His Word. I lay bare my soul in prayer, and I invite God to correct me in any area that I am going off course. I draw strength from His presence and His wise counsel. I am renewed by His words of encouragement, and I'm prepared for what lies ahead as He clarifies my calling and He outfits me with the gifts and graces I will need to accomplish His plans and purposes for my life.

If you are wise, you will make these disciplines part of your pre-plateau routine, and perhaps avoid an impending capacity overload. If you are already on the **Hit-My-Capacity Plateau,** these measures will help you recover and prepare to move forward once again.

Identifying sticking points and fulfilled capacities are critical but managing our momentum becomes more important along the journey. Our stories may be different but I am sure you'll find that there are more similarities that pertain to your context.

CHAPTER THREE

MAINTAINING YOUR MOMENTUM ON THE PLATEAU

Celebrate Hard Fought Victories, Then Move On

Climbing new heights can be exhilarating. An incredible move of God in our lives and ministries can be exactly what we prayed for. When it finally happens, well ... there's nothing like it. You may have broken records in a sales contest and won a trip to the Mediterranean, or you may have been the state champion in the 100-meter sprint as a youngster; all noteworthy and worth celebrating! Victories of the past are worthy of thanksgiving and times of worship. Throughout the first five books of the Old Testament, and into the book of Joshua, the nation of Israel (or certain individuals) would build altars to Yahweh to commemorate meeting God at that place, to remember the great and awesome miracles He performed on their behalf, or how the Lord had delivered them from their enemies. Later on, they would point out these memorial altars to their children and explain to them, "This is where the Lord gave us a great victory over our enemies against all odds!"

Genesis 12:1-9 records how Abram (later renamed Abraham by God) built his first altar at Shechem when the Lord appeared to him and promised to give Abram's descendants the land of Canaan. As Abram and his household moved south to Bethel, he built another altar dedicated to Yahweh, and he worshipped the Lord there. He settled near Bethel for a season, then he migrated further south into the Negev, and then further on into Egypt. Upon his return to Bethel many years later, Abram worshipped Yahweh once again on the altar he had built there. (Genesis 13:4) A generation later, Abraham's son, Isaac, moved from one place to another due to his conflict over water rights with King Abimelech of Gerar, and finally found a peaceful dwelling place at Beersheba. The Lord appeared at Beersheba to reassure Isaac that He would remain with Isaac and He would bless him with the same blessings that He had promised his father, Abraham. So Isaac built an altar to Yahweh at Beersheba. (Genesis 26:23-25) Years later, Isaac's son, Jacob built an altar at Bethel to commemorate where the Lord appeared to him in a dream as he was fleeing from the wrath of his brother Esau. When Jacob returned from his 21-year sojourn in Paddan-Aram, he built an altar there at the Lord's instruction, and the Lord appeared to him once again. (Genesis 35:1-10) Jacob and his family dwelled at Bethel for a season, then moved south to Ephrath (later renamed Bethlehem), and then moved on to Hebron where he re-united with his father. Upon the completion of each mighty act of God, they built an altar to commemorate what the Lord had done there on their behalf, and then set up their tents for an extended season there.

This tradition of erecting memorial altars to Yahweh continued, even down to the time of the Exodus under Moses as well as the Conquest of Canaan under Joshua. But different conditions prevailed under Moses and Joshua since the people of Israel were en route to the Land of Promise. Although they paused to build an altar to worship and celebrate what Yahweh had done for them, they near the altar only for the time it took them to worship and give thanks to the Lord, and then they continued onward in obedience to God's command.

Following the leading and guidance of Yahweh, every single one of these men eventually led their people to move on from where they had built their memorial altar, and on to the next oasis or town on their journey. They returned to worship at these sites occasionally, but the main function of these memorial altars was to declare their gratefulness for the mighty acts of Yahweh, and to share their testimony with the generations that followed after them. Through their faithfulness and dedication to Yahweh and their families, they were able to nurture and produce a legacy of faithful worshippers of the Lord.

But for those who are righteous,
the way is not steep and rough.
You are a God who does what is right,
*and you smooth out **the path ahead of them**.*

Isaiah 26:7 NLT

Pause to celebrate victories along the way. Create a lasting memory that will continue to bear testimony to God's goodness long after the original celebration is over. These memorial celebrations honor God and speak volumes to those who have been a part of the process and shared in the journey. A joyful and sincere time of praise and celebration also provide an opportunity to recite the miraculous stories of all that God has done in your midst, and they encourage the younger generation to trust the provision and leadership of God for their own lives and future.

49

Every time we have hit a major milestone at Inspire Church, we have stopped to thank the Lord and throw a party with balloons and cake to celebrate what God had done, and before we looked ahead to the next journey God was taking us on as a church! Why? Because everyone has worked hard to grow the church to where we are, and they deserve to share in the celebration and have the opportunity to share with everyone else in the church their stories of what God has done all along the way. Just remember, this is only a pause on the plateau to celebrate, not a permanent resting place. After you've celebrated, make sure you are ready to follow God's lead to move on to the next phase of your journey with Him.

> *I don't mean to say that I have already achieved these things or that I have already reached perfection. But I **press on** to possess that perfection for which Christ Jesus first possessed me.*
>
> ***Philippians 3:12 NLT***

DON'T ALLOW GOOD INTENTIONS TO DISTRACT YOU FROM YOUR GOD-GIVEN MISSION

"Let's build three shelters!" Who can blame Peter for his outburst? When something amazing happens, we have a tendency to want to relive it over and over. Just as former high school athletes often relive past victories long after their high school years are done, there is a tendency in each of us to want to replay the video of our own past accomplishments. Just as a crowd wants to bask in the glory of the moment and remain at the stadium after their home team has won the championship, the glory of the transfiguration was enough to convince Peter, James and John (and all of us) to want to stay on the mountain and bask in the moment with Jesus, Moses and Elijah.

Peter's intention to erect three tents was not completely inappropriate. It was well-intentioned. After all, the people of the Middle-East are well known for their hospitality, and Peter is suggesting that they provide proper hospitality for Moses the Lawgiver and Elijah the Prophet. In addition, a comparison of the four gospel accounts of this event suggests that the transfiguration occurred at the time of the Feast of Tabernacles (or Tents). As required by tradition, Jews built small tents or shelters in their fields or on the roofs of their homes (if they lived in the city) to celebrate Sukkoth, one of the three most important Jewish religious festivals. So instead of descending the mountain to rejoin the rest of the disciples and their families to celebrate the feast with the rest of Israel, Peter may have desired to have a private celebration with only his closest friends and his most honored guests. Again, who could blame him?

Either way, the intended purpose of building the temporary shelters was to provide proper hospitality and to entertain Moses and Elijah as their guests, thereby prolonging their visit. What Peter did not understand was that God had already given Jesus urgent instructions to begin his journey toward Jerusalem in order to die on the cross at the beginning of the Feast of Passover. Peter did not realize that all of his good intentions could possibly delay Jesus's final journey to Jerusalem and disrupt God's perfectly appointed time for Jesus at Calvary.

Good intentions can often lead to well-meaning distractions that delay us on the plateau and prevent us from accomplishing our main mission in God's appointed timing.

WE NEED TO KEEP THE FOCUS ON THE MAIN THING!

*No, dear brothers and sisters, I have not achieved it, **but I focus on this one thing: Forgetting the past** and **looking forward to what lies ahead**, I **press on to reach the end of the race** and receive the heavenly prize for which God, through Christ Jesus, is calling us.*

Philippians 3:13-14 NLT

SEVER THE ROPES OF OLD MINDSETS THAT BIND YOU TO THE PAST AND HOLD YOU BACK

Getting stuck on a plateau is often the result of a few stubborn oxen that plant their hooves in the dust and refuse to go forward. We keep feeding and placating these sacred cows that are no longer making a useful contribution and have wrapped their tethers around everyone else's ankles so they can't move forward either. Instead of forming them into holy hamburger patties set for the barbecue grill, we humor their stubborn excuses, like: "We never did it that way before;" "It was good enough for pastor … *(fill in the blank with the name of their former pastor)*, so it's good enough for me;" and one of the most overused clichés of all, "If it ain't broke, don't fix it." I call these the "Famous Last Words."

Even in New Testament times, Paul repeatedly fought against the Judaizers who wanted to carry their pharisaical past into the life of the church and impose the full requirements of legalistic Judaism on the new Gentile converts. Because all of the followers of Jesus up until the time of Stephen's martyrdom had been Jews, the Judaizers pridefully assumed that the new Gentile converts should be required to become Jews before being allowed to follow Jesus. If Peter and Paul had not persistently fought the Judaizers' efforts to tether the Christian Gospel to the requirements of the Old Testament covenant, every Gentile male would have to face the circumcision knife (ouch!) before entering the baptistery to follow Jesus.

We often begin well, as we are led by the Word and the Spirit. But when we begin to experience a degree of success and start to gather momentum, we begin to grow self-confident, rationalizing and justifying our plans to picnic on the plateau of our success. We choose to postpone our next move forward up the mountain, and we begin to rely upon the wisdom of our own experience and understanding and strength of our own flesh.

When we moved into each of our new buildings, I understood that people would have to adjust to the new setting. I thought it would be a relatively easy thing for them to do. Bigger sanctuary? Check. Air conditioning? Definitely a check. State of the art video, lighting, LED, sound system and new chairs. Check 'em all! But there were always a few people who complained that they missed the tight (and sweaty) fellowship of our first location and lamented the move out of the old, hot, rented elementary school cafeteria. I would hear, "Pastor, don't you miss the old days when we were smaller?" Me? "Uh, nope." Or, a staff member would come to me and say, "So and so says, that we've changed so much (meaning, too much!) since we moved into the new building." And I would say, "Yep! We sure have. We have begun to grow again. We're no longer crammed in like sardines in the cafeteria. We ain't sweating it out anymore in the school down the road. We are now a much cooler church!"

There will always be people who will tie themselves to the past: trying to justify and tenaciously clinging to their old mindset and old ways of doing things, trying to substantiate their convictions to everyone else. The result is that they limit the growth horizon by forcing everyone else to keep things the way things used to be, and to do things the way they used to do them. Don't let them. Pastor Brian Houston of Hillsong Church, a man I thoroughly respect and honor, along with his beautiful wife Bobbie have built one of the world's most impacting churches. While leading what was already Australia's largest church made the necessary changes that have brought about Hillsong's greatest days. I often hear him say, "I'm thankful for the past, but I'm more committed to our future." … I couldn't agree more!

Jesus had no tolerance for those who insisted on clinging to the past when God was doing something new. When some people in the crowd tried to get Jesus and his followers to behave like their religious leaders of the past,

Jesus responded, "Do wedding guests fast while celebrating with the groom? Of course not. But someday the groom will be taken away from them, and then they will fast."

Then Jesus gave them this illustration: **"No one tears a piece of cloth from a new garment and uses it to patch an old garment.** *For then the new garment would be ruined, and the new patch wouldn't even match the old garment.*

"And no one puts new wine into old wineskins. *For the new wine would burst the wineskins, spilling the wine and ruining the skins.* **New wine must be stored in new wineskins.**

(probably spoken with a tone of sorrow and impatience) **no one who drinks the old wine seems to want the new wine. 'The old is just fine,' they say."**

Luke 5:33-39 NLT

When God says it's time to get off of the plateau and begin moving forward and upward, it is time to sever the ropes that tie us to the past and hold us back. There will be some people who resist moving forward and choose to remain behind. Move on without them. Don't let them hold you back from doing what God is calling you to do. They may repent later on and run hard to catch up with you, but if you don't begin moving when God says to move, everyone will remain stuck and the ways that were fruitful in the past will become sinful disobedience that binds you and holds you captive.

Isaiah prophesied,

Listen! It's the voice of someone shouting,
"Clear the way through the wilderness for the LORD!
Make a straight highway through the wasteland for
our God!

Fill in the valleys, and level the mountains and hills.
  Straighten the curves, and smooth out the rough
  places.
Then the glory of the LORD will be revealed,
  and all people will see it together.
The LORD has spoken!"

He gives power to the weak
  and strength to the powerless.
Even youths will become weak and tired,
  and young men will fall in exhaustion.
But those who trust in the LORD will find new strength.
  They will soar high on wings like eagles.
They will run and not grow weary.
They will walk and not faint.

Isaiah 40:3-5, 29-31 NLT

For I am about to do something new.
  See, I have already begun! Do you not see it?
I will make a pathway through the wilderness.
  I will create rivers in the dry wasteland.

Isaiah 43:19 NLT

It's time to sever the ropes of old mindsets that bind you to the past, and clear a straight path in the wilderness plateau for God to lead us out of captivity into His glorious future!

As you'll see, a balanced and even-keeled approach will help us appreciate what really is important to us in the middle of it all.

CHAPTER FOUR

CHASING EXTREMES
WONT GET YOU OFF
OF YOUR PLATEAU

Looking back on Peter's statement on the Mount of Transfiguration, we tend to react two ways. (What is the second thing?)
First, we criticize his statement — his mixture of exuberant joy and
hasty miscalculation amidst his fog of disorientation. As I previously
mentioned in the account of my trip to the mountains of Peru, it is
quite easy to become sleepy and disoriented at a high elevation. But
even when we ascend much smaller peaks, it is easy to become weary
from climbing. When Peter wakes up, he sees Jesus shining in all his
heavenly glory conversing with these two amazing heroes from the
Old Testament, heroes he had looked up to since his childhood education in the synagogue. Now, barely awake and perhaps a bit dizzy
from the thin mountain air, I can imagine Peter trying to quickly
gather his thoughts, processing the entire scene before him. He grabs

for words, and then blurts out, "It's wonderful to be here! Let's build three tents so we can savor this moment, one tent for you, Jesus, and one each for Moses and Elijah."

In the presence of the Lawgiver and the great Prophet, Peter dumbs-down Jesus. He underestimates Jesus's value in comparison to Moses and Elijah. Moses may have been the Lawgiver, and Elijah the greatest among the prophets, but Jesus was the Son of the Living God. Jesus was Lord, and Moses and Elijah were just his chief servants in the Old Testament. Peter has no clue that what he is so privileged to see is a turning point in the course of salvation history. Peter, along with James and John, have a front row seat to witness the most amazing spectacle a human has witnessed since Moses met with God on Mount Sinai. In the awesomeness of the moment, the pinnacle of this humble fisherman's life, he totally misjudges the significance of the event. I really can't blame him. Under the same circumstances, I wouldn't have done any better.

When we are fully present and are celebrating on the summits of our journey, there is nothing inherently wrong with wanting to linger just a little longer. How many times have we wanted to bottle up a moment in time to preserve it for a lifetime? Since the advent of smart phones, we have the opportunity to record and capture a moment like never before. After the moment has passed and the memory has begun to fade, all we need to do is go to the photo albums on our devices and swipe away. But pictures only capture a glimpse of the moment and never do justice to what happens in real time. Peter wasn't all that much different than we are.

But life isn't always made up of breathtaking moments. Awe-inspiring moments are few and far between. For most of us, whether we are professionals, craftsmen or workforce laborers, there is a significant difference between workplace and home, labor and leisure. Personally, I cannot begin to tell you how much I love my vacation time! There are times I really wish vacation time could go on forever.

But the cold, hard reality of it is that everyday work and vacation play are vastly different from one another, and another world beckons us to return home from our vacation, get back to our daily routine, return to our jobs or callings, to roll up our sleeves, and get back to work putting a roof over our heads and food on the table.

In the time that Lisa and I have been blessed to be on this earth, we have reached heights we never thought were possible. With God on our side leading the way, we set out to do what we were called to do, and do it to the best that our human capabilities and God-given gifts enable us to do. And, we both believe that there is so much more that needs to be done! But as I have shared earlier, we've also found ourselves stuck for a while from time to time.

Since we began pastoring Inspire Church 15 years ago, we have seen periods of miraculous exponential growth, but we have also experienced seasons of plateau and decline. Social media has given all of us a platform to broadcast the highly-edited highlight reel of our lives for all the world to see. As a result, from far away, it's often easy to perceive people who are doing amazing things for God as overnight successes. We see the great charismatic couple on stage, or the entrepreneur who is blowing it up on Instagram and Facebook, and we think that they live a completely blessed and anointed life. We begin to think that they somehow have more supernatural favor than we do, that God must have just waved his hand over him or her and "voila!" Instant success!

But nothing could be further from the truth. I was so moved when I watched the now retired Kobe Bryant's acceptance speech at the awards at the ESPY's, the ESPN sports network that is the be-all and end-all of sports entertainment in the world. Now if you don't know much about Kobe and his illustrious 20-year career in the NBA, then what you're about to read may not mean a lot to you. But stick with me and hear this legend's words in your mind. "I know the sacrifices that brought me here today. We're not on this stage just because of talent or ability. We're up on this stage because of 4am. We're up here because of two-a-days (practices in one day). We're up here because of five-a-days. We're up here because we had a dream and let nothing stand in our way. If anything tried to bring us down, we used it to make us stronger. We were never satisfied and are never finished and will never be retired." And it's the same for you and me. It doesn't matter what we endeavor to accomplish or what our life goals are. They are not won and achieved by simple God-given talent or just a wave of His hand. Pixie dust from a Disney character wont turn us into what we want to be and have our dreams up until the stroke of midnight. It's so much more than that. This is a level playing field, not matter what level of talent the Lord has given you. It's about "what are you doing with what God gave you?" That's the Pound For Pound Principle. That's the Parable of the Talents.

What we don't see are the hours of prayer, the constant adjustments, and the frequent discouragement that have been overcome. What we don't perceive is their will to keep going, their courage in the face of public and private criticism, and their will to continue even while being misunderstood. Lisa and I have travailed through similar challenges and struggles over the years, but ours has been nothing like those who have already traveled so much further than us along the journey. The easy thing to do is to criticize what we don't understand and can't even begin to comprehend. But the truth of it is this: everyone, at some point in time in their journey, will hit a plateau at some point in time and each must face those challenges in their own particular and unique way with the gifts and resources that God has given them.

The differences between those who keep moving forward and those who do not are many. Here are a few things we are prone to do when we are stuck for longer than we expected. Now before I continue, please understand that ministries and businesses get stuck at various levels. For a church, it could be that you haven't passed a particular benchmark that you have been trying to reach. Did you know that the average church in America has less than 200 people in attendance on an average weekend? So many churches are struggling just to pass that mark. Within all the different ministries that serve a church, no matter what size, each of those leaders are also struggling not to peak out and plateau. The same could be said in the business world in their context. Again when it comes to life overall, that when our professional, spiritual and personal goals are attained, we can't just stop and park it there. We must eventually keep going. But better yet, we should be looking toward the future anticipating those times when we are in jeopardy of plateauing and getting stuck there, and making plans to keep moving forward.

Instead, we often start building structures on our plateaus.

We start to justify and create or adopt a theology to justify why we haven't grown beyond our current reality. Getting stuck can be so frustrating and sometimes discouraging. We try different programs or church growth strategies; sometimes they work, and sometimes they don't.

To help us explain why we are where we are at, or to avoid dealing directly with what is keeping us on the plateau, we tend to do two things. We swing wide in one of two directions. I'm sure there are more, but for this book I'm going to stick with two.

We can be at our wits end, and suddenly we hear a new teaching or experience something different that begins to resonate within us. It's at this point that we are more susceptible to adjust our theological bent and head in a different direction than we have up to that time.

One direction we might go is to gravitate toward Moses and "the Law." We can become more legalistic and sometimes over-structured. We tribe-out (congregate with people who share familiar viewpoints) with the likes of people who hold a theology that is more rigid and looks down on the gifts of the Spirit. Evangelizing the lost is deprioritized as we shift our primary focus toward maintaining and defending sound doctrine. We hold down the fort of our new (or the old presented in a new way) ideology, and we label as a heretic "whoever doesn't see it the way we see it, in the way we see it," or we accuse them of being "careless with the Gospel." In fact, we start redefining what the word "Gospel" really means to the point that it is unrecognizable and even I am confused!

At this extreme, we begin to preach that women shouldn't preach or be in leadership positions in the church. We define clear limits for the Holy Spirit's role in the church and the life of a believer to avoid the danger of fanaticism. We become critical toward other churches and choose to refuse to fellowship with other pastors in the Body of Christ over doctrine they hold or the theology we feel they are neglecting. Please hear me out: I'm not talking about those who question the beliefs of a quasi-Christian cult or another religion. I'm talking about attacking evangelical pastors who we feel we no longer have anything in common with, if we fail to see eye to eye on every subject.

When we head in this direction, we find ourselves thinking and saying things like, "God doesn't want me to be successful." Or, "God is more concerned about quality than He is about quantity." Really? I think God is concerned about both. After all, more people in church means that more people are hearing the Gospel proclaimed. More decisions for Christ means that the Kingdom of God is advancing.

In this social media savvy generation, people who react to their plateau by becoming staunch defenders of orthodoxy (as they choose to define it) are feeling more and more emboldened to get on the internet and jump on someone's Facebook page post accusatory comments. They may get on YouTube and rant against whatever "heresy" they feel like pontificating about that day. It's sad. If they chose to partner with other pastors in their area and seek their wise counsel, instead of attacking them; if they chose to devote the same energy to moving forward beyond their plateau that they are devoting to haranguing against "heresy," they would already be on the path to climbing once more. If you're here or headed toward this extreme, please, please carefully consider your ways.

Do not misunderstand me; I am a strong supporter of sound theology and structure. In fact, on our staff we have a theologian that is involved in the process of the development of our sermons every week and is present to debrief with us after the message has been preached at the first service each weekend. But when defending orthodoxy becomes our main focus, we are more than stuck on a plateau; we are building a fortress there.

If one direction is legalism, then the other direction we might go in to avoid dealing directly with what is keeping us on the plateau is to gravitate toward the extreme opposite end of the spectrum. The first extreme was hyper-Law, hyper-orthodoxy that out-does Moses and the Ten Commandments. This second extreme is hyper-Prophetic, that tries to outdo Elijah, Peter and Paul in their quest for the latest prophetic word or Holy Ghost anointing.

I believe in the present-day ministry of the Holy Spirit and the indwelling and overflow of His presence and power on my life and in the life of our church. I have been baptized with the Holy Spirit and seek to be filled and refilled again and again. I believe that the Holy Spirit wants to express Himself in our lives in a "naturally, supernatural" way, to quote my friend Pastor Brian Houston from Hillsong Church. This is the true Elijah side of things.

As we seek validation for our ongoing plateau, we search for validation of our new or rediscovered viewpoints and convictions. To stoke the fire of this new revelation we believe that we've received, we go… searching, running to this conference or that meeting. We chase after the newest move of God in hopes of bringing it back home with us. We seek after the manifestations and the signs that accompany whatever move of God is getting media attention at the moment.

Please believe me when I say that I believe and receive prophecy. I'm so grateful for some amazing prophecies that I have received and have come to pass in my life and in the life of our church. I am thankful for God's genuine messengers who have had very clear and vivid pictures of Lisa's and my future and the future of our church. And I am most grateful for the Lord who has spoken to these men and women of God who have delivered the message with clarity, and hopefully without impurities. You may know them if I mentioned their names, and if I did, you know that there were or was no guile in them. Just as hyper-orthodox legalism does not discredit the value of genuine sound doctrine, hyper-fanaticism does not discredit the value of genuine prophecy.

The extreme unbalanced reaction I am talking about is akin to the obsessed tornado chaser in the United States Midwest. It is pastors and congregations who have become more obsessed with seeking after the spectacular manifestations of God, rather than fulfill Christ's Great Commission mandate to reach people for the Kingdom of God. When this happens, we become self-focused and are more concerned about camping on the mountaintop and soaking in the glory cloud, rather than going down from the mountaintop into the valleys where the real needs are.

Even Moses and Elijah were only allowed to hang out in God's presence on the mountaintop of Sinai/Horeb for a short period of time, forty days for Moses and, apparently, only one day for Elijah, before God commanded them to descend from the mountain with a mission to accomplish.

When we choose to swing to the extreme of fanaticism to mask our disappointment over our inability to get past our plateau, we begin to embrace those things that we had previously ignored as too fringe or unimportant. Things that people would say or do in the past that we never wanted to give in to, buy into, or believe, now begin to tickle our ears and sound appealing. We begin thinking, "I guess that they were right all along." So we seek out those teachers and prophets who reinforce some of our newly embraced beliefs and obsessions.

Again, do not misunderstand me, I am all for receiving biblically-tested words of prophecy in the life of the church, but when pursuing the latest "move of God" or chasing after the upcoming prophet becomes our main focus, we must be careful not to justify our plateaued existence with seeking for more signs and wonders just as we would if we swung the pendulum in the opposite direction. After all, isn't the greatest sign and wonder the transformation of a person's heart, a person who was hell bound but now heaven destined? That is the great sign and wonder of it all—salvation of lost souls, seeing people come to Jesus and making fruitful disciples out of them.

Remember that on the Mount of transfiguration, the most important person present was not Moses or Elijah, but Jesus, the glorified incarnate Son of God. So when we are stuck on a plateau, we've got to be careful focus our attention on either the Law or the Prophets. We need to keep our focus on Jesus. Why? Because Jesus declared, "I will build my Church and the gates of Hades shall not overcome it." Jesus-- He is the author and the fulfillment of all the Law and the Prophets.

You don't have to be in ministry to do this. You could be someone in the marketplace who spends too much time away from home or someone who's so focused on losing weight or getting fit that you are caught up within another culture that pulls you away from church. You could be someone who has been blessed in business as of late but struggled in your early days; the blessing of the Lord comes for several reasons but then you're not in Christian fellowship anymore because you're busy on the weekends making money. Another example that hits home for the Kai family is that like us, your children could be of sports age and you place a value on athletics with your kids to teach them discipline and sportsmanship and, to keep them out of trouble! But Sunday's are not sacred anymore in sports and games fall on those days as well….and, before you know it, your family hasn't been to church and one of the only things that brings you back is Christmas, Easter or a family crisis and by then it might be too late. When our daughters were in volleyball clubs and tournaments landed on Sundays we made sure they were in church on Saturday evening or the earliest Sunday service. We even told the coach that they would be skipping Wednesday night practices because we placed a high value on their spiritual growth. Praise God they understood. There was give and take on both parts.

> *Therefore, since we are surrounded by such a huge crowd of witnesses to the life of faith, let us strip off every weight that slows us down, especially the sin that so easily trips us up. And let us run with endurance the race God has set before us. We do this by keeping our eyes on Jesus, the champion who initiates and perfects our faith. Because of the joy awaiting him, he endured the cross, disregarding its shame. Now he is seated in the place of honor beside God's throne.*
>
> **Hebrews 12:1-2**

What am I attempting to communicate? Balance. But more importantly, focus… focus on Jesus. In Matthew 6:33 ESV, Jesus said, "But seek first the kingdom of God and his righteousness, and all these things will be added to you." What do "all these things" mean? I believe your business, your kids, your hobbies, etc… If we seek Him first, and make His Kingdom our top priority, God will make away for us. Whether in the ministry or elsewhere, keep Jesus and Him only, as the top priority.

Peter said to Jesus, "Let's build three tents." With Jesus at the center it will help us to avoid extremes and be better able to distinguish between the different tents we have a tendency to camp in, find safety from and keep from camping out on a plateau longer than we want to be.

CHAPTER FIVE

THE TENTS WE BUILD ON THE PLATEAUS OF LIFE

Several things begin to happen when you remain on the plateau for too long. Maybe you've done this in the past? I most certainly have. Depending on who you are, your past experiences and your internal belief system, you may choose to erect a number of different tents on that plateau if you are there for too long.

THE TENT OF DELAY

We begin to build a tent of delay. Getting used to the plateau is tricky. On one hand, you don't want to stay there too long, so you definitely begin making plans for when you finally have moved on. But on the other hand, there is definitely something to be said about someone who can handle the tent of delay. So much could be said about this tent.

The Tent of Delay is the place where our maturity is further shaped. Obviously you don't want to be here any longer than necessary; however, while you are here, the best thing that we can do is to make the most of it. I know it may sound contradictory to what I've been saying thus far, but it's not. The best thing you can do during the time you spend in **the Tent of Delay** is to learn the fine art of waiting while still doing what is necessary to begin moving forward once again. One of the dangers of this tent is that we may become overly anxious about the delay.

You have dreams and visions of a brighter future. Perhaps you've been planning and hoping for something fresh and new for yourself. The intended purpose of your prolonged sojourn in this place is to develop your ability to manage your emotions while dwelling in **the Tent of Delay**.

The Tent of Delay can make you frustrated because you haven't been able to recognize yourself progressing as quickly or as far as you thought you'd be by now. You've got to be extra careful here, because you don't want to force or rush things if God wants you to learn certain skills and character attributes during your stay. Because you're not the only person involved in this process, this is where you've got to be considerate of those who share **the Tent of Delay** with you: those who are closest to you, your family, your co-workers — either those you employ and oversee or those that you work under and report to. Humility, patience and gratitude are to be developed in this tent. In **the Tent of Delay,** this is where we all need to learn as much as we can and be open to whatever God might be saying to us. There are so many lessons to be learned in the delay.

Some of God's most important servants spent a significant amount of time dwelling in **the Tent of Delay** — Abraham and Sarah, Isaac and Rebekah, Jacob, Moses, Jeremiah, Zachariah and Elizabeth, Simeon and Hannah, and the Apostle Paul all inhabited this tent in their lifetimes.

Joseph had an extended period of waiting and endured so much tribulation while he waited. From the moment Joseph received the two dreams in Genesis 37 and he began to share his dreams with his brothers, he set in motion all kinds of family dynamics that would change the course of Israel's history. Actually, Joseph's period of delay and affliction would be the catalyst for how God would fashion and set apart a special people and a nation unto himself.

David also experienced an extended delay. From the moment when, as an adolescent teen, Samuel the prophet anointed him with oil in the presence of his father and seven older brothers and prophesied that God had chosen David to be Israel's next king, it would take 15 more years before David would be crowned King of Judah and seven more before he was finally crowned King of all Israel. We will be studying this in greater detail in Part Two of this book. *(15 years for David to become King… 1 Samuel 16:1-13 > 2 Samuel 2, 3 > 2 Samuel 4, 5, 8, 10; 1 Chronicles 11:1-9, 18:1 - 19:19)*

THE TENT OF DISCOURAGEMENT

When we get stuck, one of the biggest tents we set up on the plateau is the tent of discouragement. So many people launch out into business or ministry with high hopes and great expectations. We are inspired by what other people do, and hopefully the Lord has called us to walk a similar path in life. But our dreams and plans for life and ministry rarely ever happen the way we expect them to or want them to. Because those expectations are not met right away, there will be times when disappointment will come into play.

When our plans have been delayed and we have been disappointed, the next thing that you should probably be on the watch for is for discouragement to start setting in. It doesn't have to happen this way, but it often does. And because we are human, it's quite easy for us to begin to find fault or blame in our situation. I come across this so often in other people's lives, but this has also happened in mine. We can blame a denomination for not helping us with our plans and programs. We can blame the bank for not approving a loan request.

We can blame our customers or constituents and parishioners for not making things easier for us. We can find fault with our spouses or families for not providing the different levels of support that we need in order to accomplish our goals. When we start blaming, or worse yet, when we stop caring, discouragement has set in.

In **the Tent of Discouragement**, people use words like, "I've checked out," or "I'm done, bro..." We even spout overused, loaded Christian-speak phrases like, "Oh, I'm just processing," which is just code for, "I'm upset and I'm stewing, so please leave me alone! But I'm glad you noticed I'm not happy!"

Discouragement can be a powerful enemy. We all get discouraged, but if we're not careful, **the Tent of Discouragement** could lead to worse things like **the prison of depression**. However, if we allow God to enter into our discouragement, our discouragement can become a catalyst for change. I've been in **the Tent of Discouragement** so many times, too many to count! I am grateful that one of the greatest lessons I've learned came out of one of my seasons of greatest disappointment. A season of disappointment also led us into one of the greatest new directions of our lives! *The key to benefitting during your sojourn in the Tent of Discouragement is get your heart right with God.*

A few years ago, it had become quickly apparent that we were running out of room in our church building. For the first seven years of our church, we were in a very hot cafeteria in an elementary school that maxed-out at 225 people at a time, requiring us to hold multiple services to accommodate the 700 or so faithful attenders at that time. Beginning with the 60 people who met with us in our first service in 2001, we had labored and sweated it out (literally) at that school and gradually grew to a church of 700, until a miracle happened. We were able to lease and remodel a 38,000 square foot former retail store, and we moved into this facility as our new full-time office, worship center, educational and meeting space in 2007, the pinnacle of Inspire Church's corporate life up to that time.

Financially, it was a massive stretch for us during our first year in the new building, including the million-dollar build-out (which was also a miracle at the time), but God blessed us with a season of exponential growth and we quickly went from three services to five services. We soon reached 2,500 people in average weekly attendance. We were riding high and we were so grateful to the Lord for an opportunity to lease a building in a shopping center right off one of the busiest freeways in Hawaii! As realtors love to say, "Location, location, location!" They are absolutely right.

Because we were reaching the legal capacity of our meeting space and also needed more educational space and desperately needed more parking, we began to dream about moving somewhere that had potential to reach more people for Jesus. We found 10 acres of undeveloped land in a rapidly growing community about 10 minutes west of our current location. We had plans to build a 2,000-seat auditorium to replace our 800-seat sanctuary in the shopping center. The developer loved us. A large local bank was backing us. Things really seemed like they would quickly come to fruition. We were embarking on capital raising campaigns, and we were anticipating that in two years or less, we would be moving into the most beautifully designed, technologically advanced church and meeting facility in the state of Hawaii!

Without going into all the details, just prior to our Thanksgiving holiday here in the U.S.A., we received the worst possible news, and I never saw it coming. We received an 11th hour denial from the bank's corporate headquarters in California. Because bank names, denominations, and friends were involved, it's best to refrain from mentioning anything more specific. However, initially everything looked really good, and we truly believed that everything would go in our favor. But it didn't turn out the way we wanted. I… was… devastated.

After I took about a day and a half to get over the initial shock and disappointment of the news, I needed to make a major adjustment.

The adjustment had nothing to do with forgetting about acquiring a new property or another building to lease or buy. We still needed them. The biggest adjustment that I needed to make had to do with my own heart. I couldn't afford to be upset or have any animosity toward anyone, and that especially included God. I needed to start thanking Him and trusting that He had a better plan. I needed to remind myself that He said,

> *"For just as the heavens are higher than the earth, so **my ways are higher** than your ways and **my thoughts higher** than your thoughts."*
>
> Isaiah 55:9

Romans 8:28-29 would also come into play.

> *"And we know **that in all things God works for the good of those who love him,** who have been called according to his purpose. For those God foreknew he also **predestined to be conformed to the likeness of his Son,** that he might be the firstborn among many brothers."*
>
> ***Romans 8:28-29 NIV84***

Basically, I needed to get my heart right before the Lord, and scrub it all the way clean. In fact, this is one of the greatest lessons I've ever learned in my life. The lesson is simple: I need to always get and keep my heart right before both the Lord and man in order to continue to experience His favor in my life. To do so, I need to keep my heart flexible and fresh on a daily basis. I also believe that when lessons have been learned and hearts have been scrubbed, then His "higher ways" and "all things work together" become clearer. Later on in Part Three of this book I'll share with you how God worked things out better than I could hope for and far greater than I expected!

THE TENT OF DENIAL

In this tent, everything seems fine from our perspective. "Things seem pretty good. For all intents and purposes, I think it's all good. There's nothing to worry about." Herein lies the problem. People can say that they've tried to call our attention to what's really going on. Staff members may feel like they've tried to tell us too, ... and the examples go on. An overwhelming sense of analysis paralysis seems to have taken over. Have you ever been there? I have.

The Tent of Denial is a place of inattention to the things that matter. We convince ourselves that if we can just ignore the problem, everything will be okay. It will all work itself out. But it doesn't, and it won't. You can't pretend that nothing is wrong, when everyone else recognizes that something just isn't right.

Sometimes, fear is closely associated with denial. We are fearful of that tough conversation that we need to have. We fear the reaction we might get. Or, sometimes things just seem so enormous and complex to tackle that we struggle to come to grips with all of it. So, we continue to drift along in **The Tent of Denial.** Denial isn't so much thinking, "Problems? We've got problems?" It's more of a lack of motivation to tackle the problem that we deep down know exists, but we are trying really hard to avoid acknowledging it. Inviting people into our processes helps us to see the blind spots that we can't see (or have chosen not to see) otherwise.

THE TENT OF DRIFT

As I discussed earlier in this book, I wrote about how strong currents can carry us to drift further and further away from where we started out. Sometimes, winds of change and current trends have a tempting effect on us. It's so easy to get off course from your purpose and mission, and veer off or drift off into estuaries of the larger river you were flowing in.

It could be something as simple as losing your attention span, or you have become bored with the mundane life of ministry, or the monotony of showing up for work day in and day out. I've discovered that as a general rule of thumb, the entire span of life can be broken up into ten-percent pain, ten-percent elation, and eighty-percent daily grind. I mean that for about one tenth of your life you will experience the most difficult moments and seasons you'll ever go through: the sickness and death of a loved one, marital problems or an eventual divorce that brings additional hardship to life. The next ten percent is filled with times of joy and happiness: vacationing with your family as a child, preparing for weddings and graduations, promotions at work and great times with family. The remaining 80% of life consists of the daily grind in life. Wake up, eat breakfast and work out, drive to work, work for eight hours or more, get back in traffic and drive home, have dinner, get ready for bed, and sleep… Repeat…. This is the grind. It is in the 80% of life that is grind that we are most vulnerable to dwell in **the Tent of Drift.**

Every now and then, God has his way of getting our attention when we are drifting. It could be phone call from a loved one who is concerned, or a boss who is upset because you are not meeting the quotas that he needs from you. Life has its way of "snapping us out" of our slow and steady slide into **the Tent of Drift.**

THE TENT OF DECEPTION

The Tent of Deception is the most challenging of all the tents to be in. When we are on a plateau for longer than we want to be or need to be, we are at our most vulnerable to trusting those who provide false promise of a quick and easy exit from our plateau. Again, plateaus are common and necessary. Why? Because this is where change and adjustments are implemented that otherwise would not be. It doesn't always occur this way, but when we are in **the Tent of Drift** for so long that our time moving forward has become a distant memory, and we have slid so far away from our original purpose and calling, we may find ourselves lured into **the Tent of Deception**.

As I enter my second decade of full-time ministry, I see a heart-breaking pattern that happens all too often. A person will be committed to the church, living their life for Jesus.... then, either because of job situations, troubles and trials that enter their lives, or even great financial opportunity, they begin to drift away from the church. Calls are made and texts are sent. Then, word gets back to me, or they reach out to me, and I find out that a huge error in judgment has been made. As a result, they or their family is paying a huge consequence for their choices. What happened? I believe because they had drifted so far away from God's purpose and plans for their lives, that they allowed themselves to be deceived into thinking that they would be immune from the spiritual pitfalls and attacks that were out there. They became susceptible to the traps that the enemy had set up for them. All because they drifted away. When we drift too far off course, we are in danger of being deceived. Nobody sets out in life to allow themselves to be deceived. We are not fools. But denial (pretending there isn't a problem) leads us to drift further off track than we would know, and the drift leads to be vulnerable to deception.

Reviewing my life as a Pastor and leader I can see how on a number of occasions I have been deceived—I thought it was one thing, but it turned out to be something else. I can see how I could have done better in my judgment, vet people better, be sensitive to my hunches and receive better counsel. The fact remains, I was on a plateau – in the Tent of Deception. For example, let's imagine that your organization has plateaued or it seems to be heading there. You realize that because of bandwidth, you'll need to hire some staff that can help you get to the next level. These hires are critical, because they will be able to help you shoulder the load of the incredible growth God has blessed you with over the past few years. One of the challenges you may face is that no one in your current staff clearly fits the job description you need to fill. So instead of promoting someone from within, you feel you have no option but to look on the outside.

Because you are so busy and so trusting, you don't follow up on references and past places of employment. They said all the right things when you interviewed the candidate, and it seemed to be a perfect fit. Now imagine that some time has gone by and things are not really as they seemed. The growth you hired for has been delayed. Sure, you've grown some, but there have been a few tradeoffs you'll come to unearth later.

The culture and atmosphere that you once worked so hard to create, is slowly being undermined without your knowledge. You think you should be growing more than you are, and you're wondering why some staff and even key people in your organization have slowly exited stage left or have been marginalized into the corners. Discouragement sets in. When you come to your senses (months, if not years later), you finally realize what has been taking place. You had a hunch this was happening, but not as badly as this! In fact, you had been in denial for some time. You couldn't believe this could happen in your church or your business on your watch. But it has.

You do some investigating. You dig a little deeper. You start to put the pieces of the puzzle together. When it all comes into focus, you actually get a better view of what your organization has drifted into. When you peel back the layers and review conversations you've had, you see key points in the process that should have clued you in all along. What happened? You have allowed yourself to drift into being possibly deceived.

It isn't necessarily that the person or people you hired were bad people; it's just that the enemy is an opportunist and thrives on creating discord and subtle undercurrents of disunity. He loves to seize an opportunity to take ambitions, agendas, and insecurities of individuals, and then he accentuates them to covertly, at first, then overtly, influence and tear down an entire institutional culture. How do I know this? I know this because this was our story a few years ago. It took some time to recover from our sojourn in **the Tent of Deception**, but we have struck camp and grown stronger and bigger than ever!

I took full responsibility for drifting and allowing myself (albeit unknowingly) to be deceived. Since then, we have moved off of the plateau. When you begin your ascent once again, the Lord blows over you with a fresh wind of His Spirit. There's what Bill Hybels calls, "the divine flow" that begins to well up within your staff and people. Then you find yourself like Peter, saying once again, "It's good to be here!"

A BRIEF WORD ABOUT VALLEYS

Not all plateaus are meadowlands nestled between mountaintops. Some plateaus are tablelands between a valley and a mountaintop. In organizational culture, sometimes valleys get an undeserved bad reputation. When we speak about peaks and valleys, everybody loves the peaks and summits, but we dread and avoid the valleys. Maybe it's because we see the "valleys of life" as the difficulties, the trials, and even the heartbreaking things that happen in our lives. In Psalm 23, David writes, "Though I walk through the valley of the shadow of death, I will fear no evil..." Even in sunny California, they have a place called Death Valley.

We all love to be at the top. When we think about being on the top we're reminded of the struggle, the climb, and then the glorious victory upon reaching the summit. We love to take pictures when we hit the peak — whether it's climbing Everest or K2, or simply a short day hike to the Lanikai Pillboxes or the Makapu'u Lighthouse. Both are just miles away from my home in Kailua, Hawaii.

But there's something about valleys that mountains don't provide. The soil is rich and deep in the valleys. In the valleys, you'll almost always find rivers and streams. And where there is water for irrigation, there can be crops and harvests. An abundance of life awaits us in the valleys! That's why most villages, towns, and cities are usually built in a valley or on a plateau. And roads and highways are much easier to build in the valleys to carry you from town to town, and city to city.

You can't always live on the summit of a mountain. Most higher elevation mountaintops are like deserts with thin soil or exposed rock-face and no water to drink. Only a few things can survive there for long, like the eagles and hawks that nest there, but swoop down to the valleys and rivers to find prey to feed their young.

In the account of Peter, James, John and Jesus on the Mount of Transfiguration, there was something very important at the bottom of the mountain, eagerly waiting for them in the valley.

> *As they were coming down the mountain, Jesus instructed them, "Don't tell anyone what you have seen, until the Son of Man has been raised from the dead."*
>
> **Matthew 17:9 NIV84**

"As they were coming down the mountain…" As soon as the voice of the Father had finished speaking from heaven, a freshly encouraged Jesus led all four men on the slow trek back down the mountain into the valley that awaited them below. What they found waiting for them at the foot of the mountain was someone in dire need of Jesus's attention and His divine intervention.

> *When they came to the crowd, a man approached Jesus and knelt before him. "Lord, have mercy on my son," he said. "He has seizures and is suffering greatly. He often falls into the fire or into the water. I brought him to your disciples, but they could not heal him."*

"You unbelieving and perverse generation," Jesus replied, "how long shall I stay with you? How long shall I put up with you? Bring the boy here to me." Jesus rebuked the demon, and it came out of the boy, and he was healed at that moment. **Matthew 17:14-18 NIV84**

When Jesus and his disciples arrived at the bottom of the mountain, a distraught father threw himself at Jesus's feet. The desperate father of this tormented young man begged Jesus to heal him. It is here that I find my most important lessons in valleys.

Part Two

MANAGING THE MIDDLE

I Samuel 27:1-7

CHAPTER SIX

HOW TO DOMINATE THE MIDDLE GROUND

Now that we've established how someone arrives at a plateau, and we have looked at the various kinds of plateaus that exist, let's take a look at some of the challenges and pitfalls that may occur along our journey.

One of the greatest examples of someone who navigated their plateaus is found in the story of King David. David was a shepherd boy who worked faithfully tending the family sheep. He was pulled out of obscurity and his familiar surroundings, and thrust into the limelight when the prophet Samuel anointed David to be the next King of Israel. However, Scripture tells us that although David was not the people's choice, he would be God's. Israel was more than satisfied with their own choice. The people had chosen Saul to be their king.

The people of Israel no longer valued the theocracy that God established for them during the Exodus. Rather than choosing to live their best life and thrive with the one true God as their only king, the people were more focused on what they saw all around them. They decided for themselves that they too, wanted what they perceived to be working for the rest of the world. Israel wanted a monarchy – and all of the trappings that went along with that. They desired the rule of a human king whose exploits in battle and lavish lifestyle would make them feel more proud of themselves, more self-assured as a nation.

So Israel rejected Yahweh as their king; yet, they cried out to Him and begged Him to give them a mortal king because they so desperately wanted to be just like all of the other nations around them. In their own eyes, they truly believed that having a human king would make them feel more proud of themselves and their whole national identity, and they would not have to be constantly embarrassed as a second-class nation living a severely downgraded lifestyle anymore.

God gave the people exactly what they asked Him for: Saul became the people's king. King Saul was a very tall, dark, and handsome man who was quite skilled in battle. However, this mortal monarch chose not to honor God's heart or follow the instructions given to him through the prophet Samuel. God soon regretted allowing the people to crown Saul as their king (1 Samuel 15:11), so he searched for a "man after his own heart" to become the second king of Israel.

David was merely a teenager when Samuel anointed him as next in line to be the king. He received his calling and anointing when he was about fifteen years old, and it would be another fifteen years before his coronation as King of Judah at Hebron, then another seven years after that before he would become the King of Israel. As a matter of fact, Scripture tells us that David would be anointed with oil a total of three times before he would actually become the king over a united Israel.

God's hand was on David; the favor of God was on his life. But between the three mountaintop experiences of oil being poured upon his head to anoint him as the king, there were two very significant plateaus. David's first plateau occurred shortly after Samuel anointed him in his father's house at Bethlehem. A short season of public acclaim followed after he slew the Philistine champion Goliath. Then David faced a long season as an outlaw running from King Saul, who wanted to end the anointed shepherd's life. This paranoid king was determined to eliminate any threat to his rule, and he schemed to ensure that his own son would follow him on the throne. We will look further into that account below.

The second plateau occurred after David was anointed as King of Judah. He ruled Judah from the city of Hebron for seven years while Saul's son, Eshbaal (a.k.a. Ishbosheth) ruled the ten northern tribes. This plateau was characterized by near constant warfare between Judah and the ten northern tribes of Israel led by King Eshbaal and his general Abner. It was only after Eshbaal was murdered by two of his own servants that David became the king over all of Israel.

David faced a third plateau many years after he became the King of Israel. However, it was between plateaus two and three that I find most interesting and is why I have called this section of the book, *Managing the Middle*. Of the three plateaus in David's life, this third plateau would have the greatest, most lasting impact on his life, as well as on the life of the entire nation of Israel. Having conquered all the traditional enemies of Israel, David decided to rest on his laurels and leave the fighting to his generals. He was firmly entrenched on **the King-of-the-Hill Plateau**. David did not handle his down time very well. In this plateaued season, David dropped his guard and committed adultery with Bathsheba, the wife of one of his officers. All of this occurred while David's army was away, fighting Israel's enemies. This one impulsive act began David's rapid plunge into a deep valley of sin, despair, family discord, and outright rebellion that almost cost David his throne and his life.

In the spring, at the time when kings go off to war, David sent Joab out with the king's men and the whole Israelite army.   **2 Samuel 11:1 NIV**

As king, David was supposed to be leading his army in battle; instead, he chose to remain in the comfort and safety of his palace in Jerusalem. In his place David sent Joab, his most trusted general, who had been in many battles with him through the years. While David stayed at home, Joab was leading the army of Israel on the front lines of the battlefield. The lesson for you and me? You should never delegate to others what God has specifically given to you to do.

When David was confronted by the prophet Nathan regarding his sin with Bathsheba and the murder of her husband Uriah by suicide mission on the battlefield (2 Samuel 12), he must have taken some time to reflect on how far he had come and how far he had fallen. As David looked back over his life, the defeat of Goliath was just a faded memory. As he recalled the roar of the army of Israel and the defeat the Philistines that day, what David wouldn't have traded to return to those more innocent, uncomplicated, faith-filled days. Though David had fought many valiant battles over the course of his lifetime, the boredom that ensued after becoming king and hitting the pinnacle of his military career, as well as the resulting peace that followed, would prove to be one of David's toughest battles ever.

Recently, I was in a small group of male staff members when one of the guys in our circle asked me what I perceived to be my greatest challenge in the future. I said to him and the other two men in the group, "Honestly, it's boredom." They were surprised. They either had a look that said, "Are you seriously telling us that you don't have enough work to do?" or an inquisitive look of great curiosity.

I explained to them that I believe that men are the most vulnerable when they get to their forties and fifties. I see this stage of life as a time of "convergence," as author Robert J. Clinton describes it. Men in this stage of their lives typically experience convergence, when all of the aspects of their life finally begin to work in synergy with each other, and they enter the most fruitful and productive period of their lives. Those who do not experience this convergence often become frustrated and enter into a mid-life crisis, a time in their life when they begin to ask the big questions such as:

"Am I respected by those I love?"

"What is my greatest contribution to society and my family?"

"What will be my legacy?"

"What is my true worth?"

"What really is my true purpose for being here?"

These are all legitimate questions for every person to ask during any season of life, but they are magnified during midlife when a person suddenly realizes that their life is more than halfway over. And this is normally when convergence happens. It's when it all seems to come together for you. It's when life experience and wisdom gained along the journey begin working for you and pour out of you. It's when you finally begin to touch on the financial, personal and professional apex of life. Athletes have a saying for this when there isn't a shot they can't miss, a football they can't catch or a goal they can't score that keeps them in "the zone."

> " *The blessing of the* LORD *makes one rich, And He adds no sorrow with it.* " **_PROVERBS 10:22 NKJV_**

This middle stage, mid-life, whatever we call it is not a uniquely male life challenge; women face it as well. In fact, you might be a woman reading this, and all kinds of bells are going off in your head because either you see this in your own life, or you are identifying behaviors or trends that you see in your husband, sibling, or a good friend.

I believe that what made King David vulnerable during this season was boredom. While other kings went off to war, David stayed home and slept in longer. He took naps and walked on the roof of his palace. Instead of being in the thick of the battle – rallying the troops or discussing strategies into the late night hours with his young lieutenants – David was where he should not have been (his palace), at a time (Spring) when he was needed to be elsewhere (on the battlefield) doing what he did best (leading his army and strategizing for victory).

David's extended stay on **the King-of-the-Hill plateau** led to his eventual boredom. And this boredom led him down a path to sin, deception, denial and even murder. This plateau, however, was far different from the other two plateaus David had been on. When he experienced his first plateau, after Samuel had anointed him, David was still young and hungry. He was filled with faith, and his exploits in battle inspired everyone in Israel to talk about him. In fact, he was so popular that women even began to sing songs about him. This infuriated King Saul, but David continued to do what he did best, lead the army in battle. And lead he did. He led so well, in fact, that King Saul began to feel threatened by David's success. David's many early accomplishments and victories occurred while he was a loyal and faithful leader in service to King Saul!

Please make no mistake about this: plateaus are rarely places of rest.

Normally, our time on the plateau is spent in "the daily grind" of life: steady hard work, day in and day out. Laziness is rarely a part of the plateau. If laziness begins to set in, it is usually the beginning of a slippery slide downward off the plateau into a canyon of regret! If we allow ourselves to become lazy on the plateau, we shouldn't be surprised when we find ourselves flat on our backs, looking up at the plateau from far below.

Let's look at David's first plateau in greater detail. King Saul was chasing after him. With every resource of the kingdom at his disposal, Saul vowed to "pin David to a wall." As David fled for his life, God brought him all the resources he needed. God brought him men who were looking for a real leader, and He even brought David warriors who would help defend him and keep him alive. But as you can imagine, David eventually became fatigued from being constantly on the run.

While David and his men were fleeing, they were still fully engaged as an effective army, conducting raids against enemy territories, and protecting nearby shepherds and their sheep from bands of robbers and thieves. David and his army trained together until they were a highly efficient military force. They fought enemy raiding parties against the Amalekites, who periodically invaded the land to plunder the grain harvest and capture well-fed flocks and herds. But for much of the time, David and his army were in hiding or on the run, escaping from Saul and his armies. As the days and years stretched on, Saul grew increasingly insane, and he became even more determined than ever to kill David and his men.

Saul chased after David and his men with a severely increasing vengeance. Ever faithful to God and his appointed king, David rejected the opportunity to kill Saul on two separate occasions. However, stress from constantly trying to elude capture must have worn David down.

Emotionally spent, David's judgment began to wane. The aloneness of being the one everyone looked to, the weight he carried that no one could have fully understood, began to take a massive toll. I also believe that we cannot overlook the fact that post traumatic stress disorder (PTSD) surely had an impact on David and his men. When you add up all of it: falsely accused of wanting the throne, on the run for years, battle after battle followed by more battles, it's amazing that David eventually became king! Have you ever been so stressed out that you're no longer able to make good decisions and judgment calls? David was no doubt "there."

To the casual observer, it would seem that David was stuck on his plateau. After all, the longer you are on the run, the wearier you will eventually become. But also keep in mind that David and his men were not idle; they were running raids to keep themselves alive, as well as to provide for their families. As they defended David's home territory of Judah from bands of thieves, robbers and enemy marauders, they became folk heroes in the tribe of Judah. They also formed an alliance with the Philistine king of Gath, who gave them sanctuary from Saul's military. This period of activity and waiting would be likened more to maneuvers before the top of the Sigmoid Curve (also known as the Bell Curve) in anticipation of a new peak.

In addition to the battles and other activities, David and his men were also busy raising their families. David was the leader of this band of brothers and their families. Their lives were in his hands, and they looked to him for all the answers. The pressure to provide for this formidable army, as well as the pressure to lead and protect them well, must have been immense. Through it all, David kept developing the skills he would need to rule the nation, lead them into battle, and govern them with justice. God was also refining David's character as well as growing his love for God's people. In the midst of his fifteen-year-long plateau, David was becoming more and more like a king. And yet, the ever-elusive kingship appeared to be no closer than it was over a decade earlier, the day Samuel first anointed David as king.

We spend more time in the middle than at any other place. You don't just wait. You have to do something while you're waiting. But it can get tricky. There are times that you just have to "wait upon the Lord," and not get overly anxious. I've found that at times like these, we can actually cause more damage than good when we take matters into our own hands and we try to force things to happen. I've done this to myself before. I've also employed people who didn't know how to wait upon the Lord and began to "get out of their lane." They began to force a different kind of race; either they tried to run a race that wasn't theirs to run, or they pushed to run the race before they were ready to run it. Soon it became evident that they were not only causing themselves harm, but they were also putting undue stress on our organization. They were bringing drama into the life of our entire church staff.

As I look back, I recall three separate times that this pattern emerged. Each time this happened to me contributed to my own plateau. I began paying more attention to the squeaky wheel that needed to be greased. It took my attention away from the purpose God had for us, and I spent more time dealing with a few personalities and their emotions rather than spending my time steering the whole ship.

Yes, we've got to keep growing and developing our character and skills while we are on the plateau, and we've got to work hard while we're there. But we also have to remember that no matter what happens or what we do, it is the Lord who determines when we get to move on from our plateau.

Every person is in the middle of his or her journey somewhere. You may be the middle manager who has been assured of a promotion to senior management, but it's been months since it was promised, and it hasn't officially happened yet. You may be the couple who believe you've been called to pastor a church some day; meanwhile you're serving under another pastor. You'd like to launch your church plant right now, but for reasons beyond your control, you know that it's best for you to submit to the Lord and the leadership He has placed over you regarding the right timing and the right place. The roughest part of this period of waiting is wondering whether God really is able to do what He said He would do, and having to deal with your impatience while you're waiting. Just as tough is watching time go by, and thinking you're your opportunity is slipping away. If you've ever felt that your best future seems impossibly distant, Paul assures us in Ephesians 3 that God is able to make it happen and even more.

> *"Now to him who is able to do immeasurably more than all we ask or imagine, according to his power that is at work within us, to him be glory in the church and in Christ Jesus throughout all generations, for ever and ever! Amen."*

> ### *EPHESIANS 3:20-21 NIV84*

Whatever season we are in, whatever we may be facing, God is able. He is able to fulfill the calling on your life. He is able to work through your shortcomings and setbacks. There is no stopping God from doing what only He can do. Human authorities and governing entities can't stop Him. Financial institutions or the lack of finances can't stop Him. Time and space cannot stop Him. Even the devil himself cannot stop God. In fact, God is unstoppable! However, the only person that can slow down or impede the Lord from doing in your life what He wants to do is…**you.** And in this period is when our trust in His plans and ways are challenged like no other.

GOD HAS GIVEN EVERYONE A UNIQUE DESTINY! DISCOVER YOURS! CONTEND FOR YOURS!

Every person has a unique calling on his or her life. Some would call it fate. Others call it your life purpose or destiny. I prefer to use the word, destiny. But in order to fulfill the destiny God has for you in your life, you've got to discover what your destiny is. We aren't robots designed to mindlessly obey commands. Nor are we self-driving cars that designed to autonomously navigate roads and freeways, and stop on a dime when the situation calls for it. The calling God has for your life necessitates active engagement. Our life-purpose must first be discovered so that we can each intentionally begin the journey of fulfilling all that God has intended us to be and to do in partnership with Him.

Each of us has a God-given potential that we must grow into. On that journey toward the destiny God has for us, we often make the mistake of taking matters into our own hands. When we do that, we can get sidetracked and distracted along the way. . I've heard it said that there are two important dates in your life. The first, is the day you were born. The second, is the day you discover why you were born. A God-given destiny is something worth fighting for. *If something is worth fighting for, that means there's usually going to be a great struggle to attain and sustain it.*

While I was in the multi-level marketing business at 21 years old, one of the mantras I regularly repeated was, *"There's no victory without a struggle!"* You may think that it is self-talk nonsense or like me, believe that statement is largely true. Once you discover your life purpose, that's the easy part. But the tougher part is to actually fulfill it. But it's even more difficult to determine what it is that the Lord has for you to do when you have more than one option open to you.

When I was younger, I was faced with two choices: pursue ministry or pursue business. I was frustrated because I desperately wanted to know about my future, as well as the best course of action for me to take to get there. It was a time of such personal angst because I truly wanted to know what God's will for my life was because in my heart I knew that it would be the best course for me. After Lisa and I married a shift began to happen. Lisa was working full-time for the church we would eventually be sent out from. I wasn't on staff yet because I didn't know if I was called to full time ministry or continue to run my multi-level marketing business. I've met some of the finest people I have ever known during that period of my life. For five years, it helped me to have a dream and a purpose when I did not have one. I had lost my vision for my future by the time I was 19. How tragic it was! The responsibilities of life and choices I had made up until that point; they all led me to this particular path I was on. How serendipitous is life? Looking back, would I have done it that way again? Probably not. But ask me if I'm thankful for what I've learned and been through and I will tell you *absolutely yes*. Secondly, the people I was closest to in my MLM took me to church and pointed me to Jesus. When I had no relationship with Jesus and no church to relate to, they were the ones who accepted me and became the bridge or showed me the bridge that would lead me to the Lord. Till this day, I still keep in contact with friends I made so long ago that either come to Inspire Church or I see out and about in Hawaii.

That's why it was so difficult to know what God's plan was for my life. During this stage of my life was when I struggled the most to hear His voice. I wanted to continue to persevere to become very successful in my endeavors but could sense the Lord was calling me to leave and enter into the ministry. On several occasions and in big ways, the leadership of the church made it clear that they wanted me on staff and I knew I was headed there. I had no experience. I was highly unqualified. But I was always around and had a small group that I had multiplied and reproduced several times and this got their attention, not to mention that Lisa was also employed full time by the church.

I was so sure but at the same time, I was not so sure. This was the season when I really wrestled with the Lord. A large part of it was I willing to surrender my plans for His plans. The other, *could I trust God with my overall life?* Especially when no offer had been made by the church and no guarantee. Nobody made me an offer that I couldn't refuse but nor did anyone give me an ultimatum. I was simply saying "yes" to no guarantees.

Looking back, I am convinced that this was my own Isaac that I was placing on the altar. I heard it said several times, "If you give up your dreams to God, He will replace it with something with equal or greater value." I'm not sure that it is 100% on all accounts here on earth but I am positive that it comes into play in Heaven when the

Lord hands out rewards for the deeds we have done (which isn't the same as receiving the free gift of salvation). But when I look back at what I gave up all those years ago when a huge part of my identity was wrapped up in it, I am amazed at what the Lord has done since. Simply amazed.

Who would've known that at the time (my early twenties) the decision to place something so significant in my life on the altar (my desire for business) would become the first of many that would help launch us out of future plateaus. When I finally/eventually knew that this was the course my life would take, I set out for it with all that I had. I said "Yes!" to God's call without any guarantees offered, no Plan B's and no golden parachutes. I wasn't hired right away. I had to continue to clean planes for the airlines while God prepared me for a life of ministry.

God has a plan for each of our lives. HOWEVER, our ADVERSARY wants to PREVENT us from achieving our GOD-GIVEN DESTINY.

From the very beginning, Satan has been trying to thwart God's plans and purposes in people's lives. In the Garden of Eden, God gave Adam and Eve dominion over all the beasts of the field and birds of the air. HOWEVER, God told them that they could have all that they want to eat from the garden, but what they COULD NOT have was the fruit from the tree in the MIDDLE of the garden, the tree of the KNOWLEDGE OF GOOD AND EVIL.

It is difficult for the enemy to completely stop you from achieving God's purpose for your life. However, he can sidetrack you. He can distract you. He can slow down your forward momentum. He can get us so frustrated by our lack of growth or the lack of tangible re-sults that we resort to letting down our guard and opening up our minds to compromise. He will do everything he can to get us to compromise our integrity and our ethics. That's what David would

97

do in the middle. For example, he may tempt a businessman to pay someone under the table so that he won't have to pay payroll taxes. A leader may be tempted to manipulate a situation to put him or herself in a more advantageous position, or to claim the spotlight. We are all susceptible to temptation. And David was no exception.

The Bible tells us in Genesis 37-41, that **Joseph had a prolonged waiting period** before he could enter into his destiny as Vizier of Egypt. Joseph was still a teenager when God gave him a pair of **dreams and visions** about his future. **But in the middle,** between the dreams and his ascent into greatness in Egypt and ultimately his rescue of Jacob and all his descendants, Joseph faced trial after trial during which his character was refined. He also developed the leadership and management skills he would need to oversee the collection of the surplus grain during the seven years of plenty, and the distribution of grain during the seven years of famine.

Moses also waited (and waited, and waited). Though Moses was raised in Pharaoh's palace and he received the very best education and military training Egypt had to offer, it took Moses until he was **forty years** old to recognize his true calling and destiny. **Moses waited another 40 years** between the time he first recognized his calling to rise up and deliver the people of Israel from their bondage in Egypt, and his return to Egypt to lead the Exodus. During those forty years, Moses learned the ways of the desert wilderness, learned to shepherd flocks, married and raised a family, and met with God on Mount Sinai for the first time. Even after Moses liberated the Hebrews from slavery, it took **another forty years** before they were ready to enter the Land of Promise.

The Apostle Paul spent **three years** in the Arabian Peninsula after his encounter with Jesus on the road to Damascus and his calling to preach the Gospel to the Gentiles, their kings, and the lost children of Israel. Then he spent **another eleven years** preaching and teaching in his hometown of Tarsus in Asia Minor, before Barnabas went looking for him to take him to Antioch to teach the Gentile believers about their newfound faith in Christ. And it was **another year** before the church at Antioch sent Paul and Barnabas out on their first missionary journey.

YOU MIGHT BE IN THE MIDDLE TODAY

Maybe you've been believing for the promise of God on your life to come to fruition. Maybe God spoke your calling over your life a long time ago, and you hoped that it would have been fulfilled by this point in your life, but you've had a setback, a detour, or you've hit a fork in the road that you never really expected.

Some of you might be asking yourselves why it's taking so long for your church to grow. You've been there a while, and it hasn't grown much beyond where you started. You may have a great vision for the church, but the reality does not seem to match up with your expectations. Or, you've taken that leap of faith with the business idea that you've had all your life. You're putting in long hours, developing your market niche, and trying to hire competent staff, but you don't see the results that you want yet. You might be in a job that has a glass ceiling. You can't see it, but you can feel it. People keep saying to you, "You're not ready yet. Your time will come. Be patient." And you know what? They may be right. It might even be the Lord speaking to you through them.

Your singleness is making your restless. You thought you'd be married by now. You're struggling with purity and the challenges of singleness. You're hoping and praying that the "right one" will finally come along... but you're growing impatient, and you're growing older by the minute...

I've often found that it's the stuff in the middle of the waiting that always seems to be the toughest to navigate, work through, and work out. It's the stuff in the middle. Anyone can start well, and most can finish well, but it's that **PERIOD** between the **CALLING** and the

FULFILLMENT THAT'S TOUGH. It's that **SEASON** between the **PROMISE OF A CHILD** and the **BIRTHING OF A BABY.** There's the **PROMISE,** but then there's still remains a **PROCESS** to go through to get there.

> *But David kept thinking to himself, "Someday Saul is going to get me. The best thing I can do is escape to the Philistines. Then Saul will stop hunting for me in Israelite territory, and I will finally be safe." So David took his 600 men and went over and joined Achish son of Maoch, the king of Gath. David and his men and their families settled there with Achish at Gath. David brought his two wives along with him—Ahinoam from Jezreel and Abigail, Nabal's widow from Carmel. Word soon reached Saul that David had fled to Gath, so he stopped hunting for him. One day David said to Achish, "If it is all right with you, we would rather live in one of the country towns instead of here in the royal city." So Achish gave him the town of Ziklag (which still belongs to the kings of Judah to this day), and they lived there among the Philistines for a year and four months.*
>
> *1 Samuel 27:1-7 NLT*

David was destined to become the King of Israel. He was anointed by Samuel when he was only a teenager. He was called by God out of the shepherd fields. He wasn't a common hireling carelessly wandering around with a flock of sheep. He was busy defending and caring for the family flock entrusted to him by his father. This isn't like the 1983 movie "Trading Places," with Eddie Murphy and Dan Akroyd, in which they took a bum off the street and made him the CEO of a Fortune 500 company.

David made good use of his time alone in the fields with the sheep. He developed his skills as a fighter and as a sharpshooter with his slingshot to boldly kill the lions and bears that tried to snatch away his unsuspecting sheep during the night. He spent his daytime hours playing the harp and devoted his heart and voice to singing psalms of worship to the Lord. God empowered David to become both a courageous warrior and a skillful musician. David was able to steward his time in the middle to become a man after God's own heart.

However, toward the end of his prolonged period of being hunted by King Saul, David was weary. He was tired from constantly having to be on the run. Out of fear for the lives of his family, his men, and their families, David began to make critical mistakes that could have affected his destiny. He chose to seek shelter under the protection of Achish, the Philistine king of Gath, who was one of the fiercest enemies of Israel.

From the time of David's original anointing by Samuel in his early teens to his coronation as King of Israel, was a period of about 22 years (1 Samuel 16 – 2 Samuel 10). In between the anointing of oil and the re-unification of Israel and his coronation as King of Israel, David would mature in the times of waiting. But it wasn't easy for David. As I said previously, David spent more time with the struggle in the middle than at any other time of his journey. And the middle times are when we grow and mature. But it's also in the middle, where we get bored, do things out of character and sometimes, this is where we all often "blow it."

The **middle ground** is that place between: Conception and Birth; Prophetic Promise and Fulfillment; Vision and Reality. I believe that we can maximize the middle ground if we can learn to steward well our time there.

Jesus waited until he was thirty years old to begin his public ministry. Joseph had a prolonged period of waiting. Moses waited 40 years. In fact, for almost all of the most important people in the course of salvation history, there was a period of waiting.

The middle is often a period when you can't seem to get the answers you need, when all seems quiet, but your heart is churning with emotions. Questions are on your mind and you are pleading, "Lord, when am I going to hear from you?" Some would call it the "dark night of the soul."

You've been called, but the period between when you take off in pursuit of your calling and when you get to land it and actually live it out is often a long period of time. *During this season God is actively at work in your life, though it is often unseen. He is actively developing your character, forming your values, honing your skillset, and exercising your gifts, though you may not recognize it at the time.* If your dreams, calling, vision and life purpose are not unfolding as fast as you want and need them to be, recognize that you are "in the middle." It is during these seasons of delay that we must learn to manage the middle, or our time there may be extended. It could lead you to a detour or even disqualification from your calling. And, this is the time that we have to be more alert and vigilant than ever to avoid the mistakes that many make in this period. David nearly lost everything before it all began to really converge for him.

Chapter Seven

HAZARDS TO AVOID WHILE MANAGING THE MIDDLE

Here are some things to consider when **Managing the Middle**. Remember, you don't want to just manage it; you need to own it, so you can move beyond it.

DON'T LET FEAR MAKE YOU ABANDON YOUR EVERYTHING

The Lord was EVERYTHING to David. Psalms sprung from the very core of his being. *"David kept thinking to himself..."* The New King James Version says, *"David said in his heart..."* But when David's period of life on the run gave way to exhaustion, he began to make decisions based on fear for his own safety, and the safety of those under his care. Notice that he didn't inquire of the Lord as he did before. He did not summon the priest or call for the ephod, nor did he seek out the prophet to inquire of the Lord.

*"**One thing** I have desired of the LORD, That will I seek:*
That I may dwell in the house of the LORD
All the days of my life,
To behold the beauty of the LORD,
*And **to inquire** in His temple.*   **Psalm 27:4 NKJV**

For David, this ONE THING meant EVERYTHING. After this difficult season was over, it did mean everything to David once again. We all
grow weary or drained from the battles. Every fire you put out and every
extra plate that you spin takes a little bit out of you every single time.
Storms come when we're on life's plateaus, and we can take a beating
in the onslaught. In fact, storms are common on the plateaus of life, so
we've got to be prepared for them. These are the times when we are most
vulnerable. David momentarily allowed his fear and exhaustion to cloud
his thinking, make him vulnerable, and lose sight of the ONE THING.

During the plateaus that I have experienced, there have been times
that I have harbored anxiety and allowed it to linger and affect me.
In fact, there were times when worry dominated my thoughts. We
cannot dismiss the fact that there is definitely a spiritual battle going
on. The target of the enemy's attacks when we are in the middle
ground is only 6 inches wide, the distance between our two ears. If
you don't control your thought life while you're in the middle, fear
will wear you down. It will compound the stress in your life. It will
cause you all kinds of problems physically, emotionally and spiritually, and prolong your season in the middle.

Like a teenager who got their heart broken, we replay the sad
melody of our heartbreak, worries and fears over and over again in
our minds. It becomes the melancholy background music of our plateau, and we star in our own "Little Shop of Horrors" music video.

For David, his *one thing* was his *everything*, until he let fear get
control of his mind. David was momentarily losing the battle of the
middle ground.

DON'T ALLOW FEAR AND ANXIETY DRIVE YOU TO DO THE "QUESTIONABLE"

No matter who you are, no matter how much money you make, we all need integrity. If you lose integrity, it can take years to earn back the trust you once had. It's your good name that is at stake. In the Christian faith, I like to believe that we can be quite forgiving and cut people slack for the occasional verbal faux pas or some brief out-of-character action. But when missteps become habitual, or if breaches of integrity are on a larger scale, people may eventually forgive you, but it will take them a long while to forget what you said or did, and some things may never be forgotten.

David might have received pushback from his own men when he chose to take refuge in the Philistine city of Gath. "What are you thinking? What are we doing in a place like this? Who are we aligning ourselves with?" These are all valid questions that David's men might have been asking him or even themselves. When we get desperate or fatigued we may experience lapses in judgment. What we normally wouldn't even think of doing, we find ourselves doing. Words and thoughts that are normally foreign in our everyday vocabulary become the strange message spewing forth from our lips.

So why in the world would David seek refuge in a place like Gath? This is Gath, one of the five chief cities of the Philistines. Hello? This is the city that Goliath the giant came from! What if he still has relatives living there? BIG relatives who want vengeance.

When we've been running from our enemy for a long time, taking refuge among the archenemies of our enemy may seem like a good idea. But if we're running to something that looks good and it isn't God's idea, we may be running straight into trouble or a situation that's questionable at best. David traded one persistent enemy, Saul, for the perceived safety and security of what seemed to be a lesser evil. But King Achish of Gath was also the perennial enemy of his very own people. In the short term, David's decision may have provided himself, his men, and their families a place of rest and relative safety, but would the people of Judah and Israel be able to trust him after he had allied himself with the Philistines, their mortal enemy?

At some point, David finally came to his senses. He remembered that the Lord had promised to make him the King of Israel. But this was not the time. This was not the place. This was not God's best for David. His conscience must have bothered him, so David finally went to King Achish and told him that living at Gath was a bad idea for David and his men. David asks for the town of Ziklag on the border of southern Judah. But just because he was no longer in Gath but moved to Ziklag didn't make things right. They might have been better for his conscience and possibly for his people but It was still under Gath's protection, but a good distance away from the Philistine heartland, and beyond the reach of Saul and his armies. Because of his mistaken and foolish alliance, David was still within the king's grasp, living in one of the king's towns. David was no longer sovereign; he had to obey the orders of Achish, even if it was a call to arms against Israel.

Thus, Ziklag became a place of compromise for David. Even though he was out of the city of Gath, he was still in the vicinity of what was enemy territory. When we've hit a plateau, questionable strategies and compromising maneuvers are often disguised by feigned innocence. "Oh, I didn't mean to do that." Or, "That was never my intention." Even if it wasn't we have to be careful because to many, perception is reality.

David may have submitted to the political sovereignty of Gath, but he was still in control of his decisions, and in many ways, he was still in control of his own destiny. Just a mere donkey ride about twenty miles south of Gath, David, his men, and their families settled in the town of Ziklag for sixteen months. For those 16 months, they were dependent on Achish's protection, which made them vassals or servants of Achish.

Now rewind the tape with me to the battle scene years before. Years ago, the armies of the Philistines were lined up on one side of the valley, the armies of Israel on the other. Day after day, for 40 days, the Philistine champion Goliath of Gath stood on the front line and taunted the armies of the living God. He called them out. He trash-talked Saul, the army of Israel, and their God. He mocked them and challenged them to pit their best champion against him. And all Israel could do was shout back, "We've got spirit, yes we do. We've got spirit, how 'bout you?" Like a basketball scene out of the movie *Hoosiers*.

David's father Jesse asked his youngest son to deliver some cheese and bread to the front lines for his brothers to eat. This is how armies were taken care of back in the day. David was the proverbial pizza delivery boy to the front lines. There he heard an "uncircumcised Philistine" challenge the armies of Israel and blaspheme his God. David was filled with righteous indignation, and the power of the Holy Spirit came upon him. David felled the Philistine giant with one sling-stone, and severed his head with Goliath's very own sword. His story became legendary.

Now fast-forward with me to David at Ziklag, a Philistine town governed by the King of Gath. David and his men are no longer in Gath. David asks King Achish, "If it's alright with you, we'd like to move to the town of Gath instead of staying in the royal city." So the king agrees and allows David and his men to settle in Ziklag and they do so for 16 months. I believe David began to question his decision of staying in Gath. It might have weighed on his consciences a bit more. Perhaps he felt better if he got them all out of Gath but took them to Ziklag instead. Maybe Ziklag is supposed to be more acceptable. Perhaps he could rationalize and justify Ziklag more than he could Gath. Ziklag becomes that middle ground on the plateau and we begin doing questionable things because we are either bored, we are forcing the situation to get us off a plateau or we have lost good judgment like David did. Okay, I think we get the idea. Ziklag: "At least it's not Gath. It's only Ziklag." We rationalize our decisions. "Besides, what happens in Ziklag, stays in Ziklag." This is where David and his men were. And later they would pay a dear price for it. Don't let your fear and anxiety lead you toward compromise and do the QUESTIONABLE. Because of David's exhaustion and impatience, he was on the verge of making one of the biggest miscalculations on his inevitable journey to the throne.

Chapter Eight

TRADING KINGDOMS

If someone were to promise you a trip to Disneyland as a kid, but just a week before your trip a carnival came to town, how would you respond?

Growing up in rural Hawaii was an amazing experience I would not trade for anything. I grew up in the little town of Pahala, Hawaii just about an hour's drive from the Big Island of Hawaii's biggest town called Hilo. Back in the mid-1840s and 1850s, Hilo was the epicenter of Christianity in Hawaii. According to Christian historian Elmer Towns, Hilo was at the center of the Hawaiian Great Awakening. It was one of the world's great hotspots of Christian revival! In this now sleepy, coastline town, Hilo had grown up around the Haili Congregational Church, the largest church in the world at that time. Haili Church, pastored by the missionary pastor Titus Coan, met in an open-sided *hale* with over 7,000 people in attendance each week. Haili Church had a membership of up to 10,000 native Hawaiian people who would travel by foot and by horseback for hours from neighboring towns and villages just to attend church and hear the Gospel preached. Towns lists the Hawaiian Great Awakening that took place in Hilo and the rest of the Kingdom of Hawaii among the world's Top Ten Revivals in history!

Pahala was just an hour away. I didn't know the history of Christianity in Hawaii at the time, but I did know that there was a God and that His Son was Jesus. I served as an altar boy at the Pahala Catholic Church under a great priest and shepherd I have always looked up to, Father Hyman. With a God-consciousness due to my Catholic upbringing, having received my first Holy Communion at the age of eight, I would serve almost every Sunday morning as one of two altar boys dressed in my black robe and white cassock. I looked very holy and cherub-like back in those days! I hope that hasn't changed too much!

It was late in the month of May, and my third-grade year was coming to an end. What signified the beginning of summer was the carnival that was slowly being set up in the baseball field behind the school. Everyday, something new was being assembled. From the Octopus with its curved black arms, yellow light bulbs that served as suction cups, and the two-person compartments at the end of eight large tentacles that rotated 360 degrees as each arm would lower and raise, to the towering Ferris wheel, the carnival was coming taking shape. The next day, all of the concession stands of cotton candy, teriyaki beef sticks, and popcorn sprung up along with the gaming tents of darts and balloons and Coke bottle ring tosses. Stuffed animals and huge rainbow spiraled lollipops were being hung from the tent polls to entice adults and children alike to trade in their dollars and coins for scripts. Every day, I begged my parents to let me go to the carnival for just a couple of hours to get it out of my system. Each time, my parents said an emphatic, "No." They were not being cruel, but were actually being very generous. Because, in just one week my parents were going to be taking us to Disneyland!

For several years, Mom and Dad had saved up enough money to be able to take all four of us kids on a three-week trip to California, then through Oregon and on up to the great state of Washington. We were so excited we could hardly contain ourselves when Mom and Dad gave us the news. We were the most thrilled about going to Disneyland's Magic Kingdom. We knew we would also drive through Yosemite National Park and see the incredible, majestic redwood forest. We knew we were going to San Francisco where we would catch the Amtrak train that would take us further north to Seattle, Washington. But none of this could compare to visiting Mickey Mouse, Donald Duck, Jiminy Cricket and the rest of the cast of characters that Walt Disney had originally created with just a pencil and some paper.

As the Ferris wheel was being set up, I resolved in my heart and said to myself, "I will go and enjoy myself at this carnival." I'm not proud of what I'm going to say right here, but this story is true. It is now long past and it is what it is. For the next couple of days, I had begun to embezzle two extra quarters each day in addition to the quarter I needed each day for my lunch money. By the time the fourth day came around and the carnival opened, I had amassed a small fortune of two dollars (It was the mid-1970s, and two dollars still went a long way back then). It was just enough to give me a little taste of the carnival and get it out of my system so that I could focus more clearly on what lay ahead on our trip to Disneyland.

So on that day late in the month of May, I took my money and ran out the back door. I ran through the yard and under the two mango trees, then to the top of the embankment to the bottom of the chain-link fence. I climbed up the high fence and jumped over to the other side. And there it was before me, our own miniature magic kingdom, the Carnival! I would have to make this fast, I thought to myself. I ran straight to the script booth that stood just outside of the gaming tents. The attendant handed me the scripts in exchange for my quarters. I knew exactly what I would hit first. I went straight to the strongman test and picked up the sledgehammer after turning in a couple of scripts. I lifted it as high as I could, then dropped it on to platform with great force, but it barely lifted the lever and rose pitifully short of the bell. I remember feeling disgusted with myself, so I ran straight to the attraction that I wanted most of all.

Deep in the middle of the carnival was the clown-faced jumping balloon. To enter you needed to lift up the nose of the clown and begin walking on a canvas filled with air that gave you a sense of weightlessness. I began jumping inside the balloon with great delight, even though I also knew that this wasn't right. I tried to do a somersault, but when I landed, my forehead hit my knee and opened up a gash over my right eyebrow. I... saw... blood. I began to panic. So I jumped out of the balloon, put my flip-flops on, and began to sprint toward home. The problem was that as I was running through the field, away from the carnival, I saw my mother and brother out of the corner of my eyes in my peripheral vision. They were standing in the parking lot of the school. Just then, my brother began yelling out my name, "Michael!" I pretended I couldn't hear them and kept on running. My justification in my eight-year-old mind was that "If I don't acknowledge you, then you do not exist and this is not happening."

I got to the chain-link fence. I climbed up and jumped over to the other side. Without skipping a beat, I ran down the embankment under the mango trees, through the backyard and into the back door of our house. I ran through the kitchen, down the hallway, and into the bathroom, where I pushed myself up on the sink counter and stared into the medicine cabinet mirror. There was indeed, blood. Lots of it! I tried to stop the bleeding, but the gash would not close. There was blood all over my shirt, so I took it off and stuffed it in the back of the cabinet under the sink to hide it. I put on a fresh shirt, and that's when I heard my mother's Volkswagen van pull into the driveway.

"Michael!" Mom marched into my bedroom where she found me lying on my bed, casually reading a comic book. "Michael, why didn't you stop when I called you?" I lied and told her that I didn't know what she was talking about. Even more emphatically she said, "Michael, your brother and I both saw you running through the park. Now tell me, what were you doing at the carnival?" Without skipping a beat, I asked her, "What was I wearing?" The look on her face was incredulous!

What amazes me even more is that I was willing to risk it all, even the fun and adventure of Disney's Magic Kingdom in just a few weeks, for a cheap, scaled down version of it known as the neighborhood carnival. The things I said to hide it. The things I did to make it happen. It still blows me away that my conniving little mind had the ability to think on my feet and lie about things so easily.

In the garden, Adam did the same. Even David did uncharacteristically devious and reckless things in times of boredom and under times of pressure.

My Dad came home within the hour and Mom told him everything. I recall him walking slowly to my room, with the creek of his leather shoes and leather policeman's belt (Dad was a police officer for almost 20 years prior to moving to a job in the private sector). I knew I was in for a meeting of leather on skin. Without going any further into the story and sharing my parents' disciplinary practices, let's just say that I had a "Come-to-Jesus moment" that afternoon.

They nearly canceled the trip that day; until I sang like a canary and told them everything about it: the embezzlement, the strategy, the insider trading and infiltration practices of getting into the carnival before it actually opened to the public (just kidding about the insider trading). It's amazing just how much leverage a father can exert on an eight-year old delinquent when he tells that son he will stay at home with his boring grandparents if he doesn't come clean!

Till this day, it still befuddles me that at even such a young age, I was foolishly able to rationalize pursuing a lesser kingdom that was close at hand; and that as a consequence, I nearly missed out on a far greater kingdom that held so much more promise.

Isn't it amazing how our fear and exhaustion can cause us to forget who we are and whom we serve, leading us to make decisions without considering their possible consequences? That's precisely where David found himself. There was a greater kingdom that was a part of his destiny. It was somewhere in the future, and he was getting closer to it. Yet, he had to keep running for his life as Saul doggedly chased after him and provide protection and security for his men and their families. Everything converged into a perfect storm that led David to make a decision that could have turned out to be a huge mistake.

This is why we can't get impatient on the plateau. We've got to remember that God is working all things for our good. There's a level of trust that increases when the Father makes a promise. How many people have quit just before their promise came to pass...

But David wasn't just going where he didn't need to be. David became what he never thought he would ever become. Not only did he choose to live in a place he never thought he'd live, he also chose to do the unthinkable. He made an alliance with the archenemy of Israel.

When David realized the potential consequences of his decision, he tried to salvage his reputation among the people of Judah. While living in Ziklag, David and his men tried to maintain favor among the people of Judah by going on raids against the Geshurites, the Girzites, and the Amalekites (enemies of Judah who still inhabited part of their land and its borders). They plundered their camps and cities, then killed everyone so that no one was left alive to reveal where David had actually been raiding.

Meanwhile David deceptively told Achish that he had raided and plundered several portions of Judah. He wanted to convince his Philistine overlord that he was no longer loyal to his own people.

David's fear-induced decisions had the potential to jeopardize the destiny that God had planned for him. David had to take drastic measures to realign his heart with God and reclaim the destiny God had for his life. He needed to step away from the cliff on that middle ground to keep him from plunging over the plateau into a quick and steep decline.

Chapter Nine

POOR CHOICES THAT CAN SIDETRACK YOUR DESTINY

There are two critical questions to consider during this stage: whose agenda are you following, and who are you aligned with? A great friend of mine, David McCracken, recently reminded me that if you have to keep asking yourself about whom you should align yourself with and you have to convince yourself that it really is the right choice, then you've probably made the wrong choice.

Gath represents a place that you would not go to. "Oh, I would never go *there.*" But *there* may not be as questionable as, let's say, a Ziklag. But let's be honest; it's close enough. As I've mentioned before, *there* does not have to be a geographical location or a pin on your map. It could be a philosophy, a perverted ministry principle, or even a questionable practice. Sometimes we can posture and position ourselves to be aligned with the right people who can hopefully help us get to all the right places. There is nothing inherently wrong with this. Denominations, business organizations, and brands do this all the time. Networks, associations, and movements get created, and as the title of Thomas Friedman's best selling book title says, *The World is Flat*.

When choosing alignments, I must always remind myself that my alignments must be God-breathed and God-ordained. Not my agenda, but the Father's agenda. Oh, I definitely have my own agenda. My agenda is to be everybody's best friend. I love people. And there is also an insecure part of me that wants to be loved by everyone. My own insecurities can get me **in trouble**.

Secondly, we must learn to be keenly aware of our own agenda. Agendas are, basically, motives that eventually come to light. Agendas are important as we choose whom we will align ourselves with. Our alignments influence and steer our agendas. David's agenda, which included moving himself ever closer toward the throne while protecting himself from Saul, helped him decide his future alliances. The disturbing element in this story is that King Achish had his own selfish, calculated agenda in offering sanctuary to David: "Achish believed David and thought to himself, "by now the people of Israel must hate him bitterly. Now he will have to stay here and serve me forever!'" 1 Samuel 27:12. Interestingly, while David was trying to deceive Achish regarding where he had been, Achish had a plan for David as well. Who was playing whom here?

What are some of the lessons we can learn from David's brief hiatus into not managing the middle well? Here are two important things I want you to consider:

FAITHFULNESS HAS A PAYDAY

Faithfulness — There's going to be a day when you'll be able to cash in your faithfulness. There's going to be a time when all of your hard work *in the middle* will pay off. There is an appointed time.

There are two words for "time" in biblical Greek. The New Testament was written in Greek, the language spoken throughout much of the world at that time. The first word for "time" is, *chronos*, the root word for "chronology." *Chronos* is time measured in seconds, minutes, hours, days, weeks, months, and years. The other word for "time" is *kairos*. *Kairos* means "appointed time" or "opportune moment." In the Bible, *kairos* is always based on God's timing.

But here's the catch: you don't know what that time is. ***It might not yet be your time, but eventually it will be your turn!*** You are called to remain faithful. Keep doing the work of the ministry. "Don't grow weary doing good." When we believe that "God is taking too long," those are the times we begin to make reckless, unwise compromises.

What do we do in the meantime, while we're on this particular plateau of life? We should be actively participating and partnering with God toward the fulfillment of His destiny for us. At the conclusion of the parable of the talents in Matthew 25, Jesus says that if He finds that we have been faithful in the little things, then He will entrust us with greater things.

In my previous book, *The Pound for Pound Principle*, I wrote about what that kind of faithfulness entails. Let me just say that basically, faithfulness is doing the best you can with the opportunities, resources, time, and gifts that you have been given by God.

Patience — Bucking up against authority and boundaries that have influence over us never helps. It only hinders. Being a self-proclaimed go-getter myself, sometimes it's difficult to remain patient. The last thing we want to do is to get outside of God's will, as well as outside of His timing. Many people, out of frustration and impatience, have either pressed the pressure release valve of the work that God was completing in their lives to take them to the next level, or they forced the issue for things that they were not prepared to step into and assume responsibility for, or they forfeited the opportunity to let God bless them with His best.

Contentment — Contentment has to do with knowing who we are. Just as important is knowing who we are during the season in which we are currently living. The person who is always trying to find themselves or always trying to find out who they are, will be riddled with insecurity. When we are insecure, we lose our contentment for the season we're in right now. Plateaus are supposed to build character. And a large portion of that character-building process shapes who we're becoming while we wait **in the middle**. In fact, I think you can take full advantage of your plateaus be studying them. Look at how you arrived there. Debrief with close friends and associates that can help you ascertain as to what to look for in the future to avoid another plateau if at all possible.

Toward the end of his plateau, David was becoming a worse version of himself rather than a better one. Fortunately, he had not yet forfeited the call of God in his life. We all know that it was a different time in a different era, and things were done differently then. Men inevitably went to war. And people inevitably died in battle. This had to have weighed heavily on David's heart. When we lose our contentment in the place where God has us at that particular moment, our thoughts and actions become even more critical than ever before. Time spent learning great lessons on this plateau can become time squandered if we fail to learn these important lessons. This can result in extending our stay on that plateau. A lack of contentment basically says, *"God, I don't like what you've given me."* And when we lose contentment, we lose another great attribute that God loves, gratefulness. Yet at one point in David's journey, he was able to say,

> *"LORD, you have assigned me my portion and my cup; you have made my lot secure. The boundary lines have fallen for me in pleasant places; surely I have a delightful inheritance."*
> *Psalm 16:5-6 NIV*

David knew contentment and gratitude for much of his life, and he practiced it often. But he momentarily let go of his contentment and gratitude when his plateau of running from Saul continued past the limits of his patience and wore him down.

Diligence — Hard work, as we discussed earlier, is an essential part of pursuing our destiny. Whenever we are on a plateau, it is not the place to be kicking up our feet and serving ourselves up a tall, cold one. Those are called vacations, not plateaus. A plateau is not a vacation, nor is it a sabbatical. When waiting for a new assignment, there are important things that God is doing. He is purifying of our agendas. He is narrowing our alignments to those that honor Him. This is an important place to stay busy doing the right things. Right actions, right habits, and right results will ultimately lead us to a right destiny. It's that simple. When on a plateau in life, stay in your lane and do what you are supposed to do.

DON'T BLAME OTHERS WHILE YOU'RE ON THE PLATEAU:

One of the common mistakes we make when we're stuck and haven't moved on is to blame others for our predicament. It could be the economy or a boss who hasn't promoted you. The scapegoat might be an uncooperative spouse or a seemingly overprotective parent. The list could go on. Being on a plateau can be quite precarious. Here are some dangers, pitfalls, and traps to be aware of.

Cynicism — Our outlook and perspective taints the way we see things. We quickly dismiss and discount, or even dumb down what other people have accomplished in their lives. This comes out of a perceived lack in our own self-worth and is often rooted in old feelings of rejection from our past. Everything that is alive and surfaces has a root. Many of our default responses are attached to the root of cynicism. Again, as we discussed earlier, contentment in God, an understanding of who He is, and how He has uniquely designed us for our destiny can help crush this bitter root.

Jealousy — We covet what other people possess, not realizing the price that they've paid. We are most often jealous of very gifted people with the perceived favor of God on their lives. Whether they're in business or in ministry, they have a way of making things look easy. Sure, it's easy to look at someone else's accomplishments and think to yourself, *"if I were in his shoes, I would be crushing it."* Or, *"This is all the favor of God and nothing else. If God could speak and use Balaam's donkey, then he could use this guy I work for..."* When we experience plateaus, it's easy to rationalize away someone else's fruitfulness and success.

Sadly, I've often seen this jealousy cloaked in a spirit of religion or religious language that sanctifies their lack of success at the moment in order to gain a superior and self-righteous edge over another person's accomplishments. They'll use phrases like *"as long as you're becoming more and more like Jesus..."* Although it's true that we should be conformed to the image of Christ, this phrase, and those like it, can be a type of dismissal of the value of their success, and a suggestion that their character has somehow been compromised in the process of becoming successful. This life is full of people who regularly recite their "coulda, shoulda, wouldas."

The reality is, a high price has been paid by these successful individuals that most people will never know about. Humble and successful people rarely talk about *the price* they've had to pay. Do you know why? Because they're afraid to touch what I like to refer to as "the Ark of God." I'm referring to the scripture passage in 2 Samuel 6 where Uzzah reached out to steady the Ark of God when it was being wrongly transported on a cart from Abinadab's house to the City of David. The Ark was being transported on an oxcart, rather than carried on the shoulders of the priests as specified in Numbers 4:15 and 7:9. It began to fall, and with great intention in his heart,

Uzzah put his hands on the Ark to steady it, but he was struck dead. Why? Because no one other than the priests was allowed to see or touch the sacred articles from the Holy Place, including the Ark of the Covenant (Numbers 4).

Every time someone feels that they have to defend God's blessing and favor on their lives, it feels like they're touching something sacred to them, because they understand it is an act of God's mercy and grace. If there is ever a time I feel that I need to back myself up or justify what I've accomplished, I feel like I'm touching the Ark. I know that it's sacred.

There is a fragile balance between recognizing the blessing and favor of God on your life, and stewarding it well in partnership with God. I don't take a laissez-faire attitude or take for granted God's blessing on my life for one moment. I don't think I deserve it. (None of us do.) But I also know that I have paid a high price, having received it. So have people who have worked for and with us from day one and all along the way. There are rare occasions when I have to justify the success of our church and what I have accomplished. And when I do, I know that it must be something serious. Or, someone has got my goat enough that I felt that I had to go there and I've been placed in a defensive position that makes me somewhat aggressive and assertive.

Mockery — David's wife, Michal, mocked him for rejoicing as he finally brought the Ark of God to the place he had prepared for it in Jerusalem. She sarcastically belittled him for his fervent, worshipful expression and excitement for God and accused him of strutting his stuff naked for the maids of Jerusalem. The Lord caused her to remain barren for the rest of her life. (2 Samuel 6:14-23)

I wonder how many times God's intention for supernatural impregnation of dreams and visions may have been delayed until someone repents of their mockery of God's servants and their expressions of devotion to God. I also wonder if those who judge someone else's actions and misinterpret their zeal for God would be so quick to find fault if they were suddenly and divinely blessed in ways beyond their reasonable explanation. I am sometimes guilty of this. May the Lord forgive us for our jealousy and ignorance when we fail to recognize and celebrate all that He is doing in another person's spiritual journey!

Desperation and Despair – This pitfall is one that we need to be extra careful to avoid. Desperation and despair sometimes cause people to self-medicate with sex, drugs and alcohol, or they become so frustrated that they pull other people into their plateau with them. I've had brief flirtations with the Double D's. I've also been here before with some of my closest friends and relatives.

I've seen the Lord use desperate circumstances to get people's attention. Why? Because He loves us. There are lessons that He's trying to teach us, and intimacy that He's trying to nurture in our relationship with Him. At the end of the day, the Father wants us to be close to Him. When we're faced with desperation and despair, that is precisely the time that we need to draw near to God, and not distance ourselves from Him.

Our spiritual formation can kick into overdrive when we're facing desperation and despair. In our desperation, God will meet us right where we are, and He will work to re-create us in the image of Christ. He will also continue the good work to re-create us into His best version of ourselves. For God, it's not about who we are right now, it's about who He desires for us to become.

We often call the season in which we are most likely to face desperation and despair our "midlife crisis." Others call it "halftime" — that stage of life when we are worrying and wondering what the next few decades will look like for us: financial security, self-fulfillment, life achievement, legacy and completion of our divine assignment.

Blame and Bitterness – When a person has handled their plateau poorly, they start to look for people to blame, and open themselves up to a root of bitterness. The blame game circumvents our need for introspection during this season. I touched on this briefly at the beginning of this section. When we head straight for the blame route, we stop looking for the answer or cause in our own life. The finger is pointed outward and not inward. This is where mirrors begin to fog up and we no longer get a clear view or assessment of what's going on inside. We start "venting" our frustration and anger at others. We begin recruiting people to take our side, and suck them into the vortex of our pity parties. We form our battle lines and lob volleys of blame and innuendo as we attack other people's character and actions (or inaction). Everything becomes quite dangerous at this point because we have left the plateau of struggle and challenges and descended into the pit of sin: gossip, slander, character assassination, malice, bitterness and hatred. In the blame game, any and all of these tactics are highly destructive. It may undeservedly harm the reputation of the person you are blaming. It causes disunity and division in a church or on a business staff or sports team. It robs us of valuable time and energy, including the time and energy of those who rally to our side. And it can even rob us of our physical, emotional and spiritual health.

In Proverbs 4:23 NLT, the bible tells us, *"Guard your heart above all else, for it determines the course of your life."* It's times like these that we've got to be careful to guard our hearts and not let it get into our spirit. Blame and bitterness, desperation and despair makes us all vulnerable to the enemy's subtle attack on us. It's at times like these that we have increased our exposure (to use a legal term) and the devil would like nothing more than to derail us over heart issues.

Loss of passion — Due to discouragement and frustration, the desire and passion for your current assignment often begins to slide.

We begin to lose our sense of purpose and the passion we had for what we did in the first place. Even if we are not currently employed or engaged in doing what we love to do, as followers of Christ, we should be giving everything we do our best effort. Why? Because ultimately, we work for God. Whatever we do, we should do it as unto the Lord.

One of the best ways to maintain your passion is to gather with other believers for weekly support and encouragement. Our church calls them Connect Groups. Others call them Life Groups, Care Groups or Mini-churches. Can I warn you that this group is not the place for you to vent all of your frustrations, especially if it involves naming a specific individual? You've got to be very careful here. Though confidentiality is often preached, if your plateau involves people, may I advise you to be very selective about what you share and with whom you will share. Our groups can quickly become fertile ground for the enemy to cause people to take up each other's offenses, and people may, at times, begin to breed their own judgments and offenses even if they had no intention of doing so. Sharing our hurts and prayer requests can quickly be turned by the enemy and transformed into character assassination. If we are not prayerful, even the slightest and softest wrong intention can leave a bad odor that lingers in the room long after you have left.

There were times that I couldn't wait to get away from where I was to where I needed to be. As I said earlier, my heart was one of the things I really needed to be diligent about. Every time I get frustrated over things not falling into place for me I needed to constantly remind myself that if I did the right things, the right way that God would have my back. Lisa would always remind me as well. I have great friends in the ministry I can always call. I've been blessed with "older-brothers" in the ministry here in Hawaii, on the U.S. mainland and internationally as well. They've all been on the journey a bit longer than I have and always have incredible wisdom to impart and a listening ear to lend. I'd say if you have a few of these, friends and brothers (or sisters for that matter), you'll do just fine. Without them, it's very possible that I could have tripped over an offense or allowed my heart to go bad. And, times on plateaus would be prolonged.

CHAPTER 10

WHAT CAN PROLONG YOUR TIME ON THE PLATEAU?

What can keep us on our plateau longer than necessary? All of the above-mentioned pitfalls can circumvent our growth while we are on our plateau and prolong our time there, and we will stay there as long as necessary to learn all the lessons God has for us. We cannot expect God to move us into a place of promotion after a poorly handled plateau.

The perfect example from the book of Genesis is Esau, the son of Isaac. Rather than embrace his role as the eldest son of a tribal chieftain, he preferred the life of an outdoorsman. He chose a pagan wife to satisfy his carnal appetite, rather than one who would help him pass along the faith of his fathers to future generations. He poorly managed his plateau of young adulthood as he waited to take charge of his father's sizeable household, flocks and herds. As a result, when he came in from the fields famished one day, he sold his birthright (a double portion of his father's inheritance) to his younger twin brother Jacob for a bowl of lentil stew. Then Esau lost his patriarchal blessing to Jacob when he proudly offered to hunt down his father's favorite game before being blessed. Esau's mismanaged plateau resulted in a life spent wandering as a herdsman on the other side of the Jordan. His descendants followed in his footsteps for centuries to come.

From my years of experience in ministry, here are a few additional things that can keep us on the plateau longer than necessary.

1. Discouragement

Every time you either make a change or change has been thrust upon you, it invariably comes with a price tag. Of course these will often impact your personal relationships. Your professional adjustments spill over into your personal life. A few ways that discouragement can enter into the scenario are:

- There is disappointment when changes take place or transition is not implemented the way we envisioned it would happen. My good friend, Dr. Sam Chand, counseled me regarding the difference between "change" and "transition." As Dr. Chand says, change happens at the moment it is implemented, while transition is the period of adjustment. Change is matter-of-fact, while transition involves people's emotions. We were excited to plan the opening day service for one of our new locations. As the day approached, it was necessary for me to change the role assigned to one of our pastors for that special service. The staff pastor understood the change, but it took awhile for the spouse to come along. Change will often involve family members of those whose roles call them to be flexible. But it was obvious to me that the spouse was wrestling with my decision. Dr. Chand told me that mentally, *she was already picking out the dress she was going to wear, pondering where she would stand, and how they would minister together.* He made a great point. Change happens, but it rarely happens the way we see it happening, and sometimes details don't pan out as we hoped they would, and this can cause discouragement. The emotion was eventually overcome and she came to understand the necessity for the change and we all live happily, ever after!

When we implement changes, it is important that communication is clear and leave no room for misinterpretation. The devil loves to get in the details so he is always active to create confusion and capitalize on misperceptions. That's why it takes hard work and loving care to keep people "in the loop" and receive information first hand about what will likely affect their lives for a while and it is particularly noticeable in a fast-paced, fast-changing organization. There are so many conversations to have and emotions to process that during a season or period like this that there is extra TLC applied. I'm always reminding my staff that we should always be mindful to circle back on tough conversations we have to clarify our positions and summarize our conversations if need be. Always try to make sure that both parties are in agreement of what's been said. This takes more time but it can remove any confusion because 1 Corinthians 14:33 KJV tells us that "God is not the author of confusion" so it takes finesse to have these tough conversations.

Discouragement has far-reaching effects that will not only impact your own life, but also has the ability to be broadcast to others. A friend once explained it this way: people are either "lightning rods" or "conductors." A lightning rod will take and receive powerful information and be able to ground that information. What comes to them, stays with them. Conductors take that same powerful information and begin to broadcast and distribute all they receive...and more.

The "lightning rod" is that devoted friend who will intercede for me and seek the Lord on my behalf. He knows how to effectively help me process the issues and challenges I am currently facing. That

131

lightning rod goes straight to the source of the problem, and grounds it there. He seeks the Lord, the source of all knowledge and wisdom, and then he is able to give me wise counsel on how to best follow through to God's best in the situation. This is the healthiest way to support and encourage a friend, and help them work through their problem, issue or challenge in the best possible way. People love hearing information and love broadcasting it. Thank God for the lightning rods in your life. Proverbs 18:8 in the ESV puts it like this, *"The words of a whisperer are like delicious morsels; they go down into the inner parts of the body."* So be careful of who you confide in.

There are few things more dangerous in the life and well being of a business, church or organization than a discouraged and disgruntled person who connects with a "conductor" to spread that discouragement through the whole organization. That is why one of the main refrains throughout this book is, "Guard your heart."

In "guarding our hearts" we've not only need to be vigilant over what we allow in us but we must also be able to process the information given to us so that when others are stuck we can console them correctly.

Even more critical in our communication with others is this: we must always be mindful to carefully inspect our own hearts, minds, and attitudes regarding what we share and how we share it with others. What goes in, comes out again. It is often reflected in what we say and how we say it. That doesn't mean you can't say anything to anyone when you're facing discouragement, but it does mean that we need to be mindful of our choice of our words, as well as the tone and attitude we use to express what we're saying. That will make all the difference in how our communication is received, perceived, processed and understood.

If you are in a leadership position and there are individuals in your organization who become discouraged because of change and transition, take the time to develop the necessary valuable skills to sincerely and effectively help them. Support them in their growth, help them to be able to recognize their discouragement and pain, and guide and shepherd them through the process. Learn to call out the best in them, speak encouragement into their lives, and help them to reclaim their destiny.

2. Character Issues

Spiritual formation is one of the principal purposes for your life on the plateau. Growing spiritually with God as you acquire and learn to steward well your new skills, gifts, wisdom and knowledge, is essential to living the life God has planned and purposed for you every step of the way. Your ability to succeed and thrive in your new season is one of God's main goals for you. He is actively involved in growing your relationship with Him as you partner to develop the character of Christ in you. Our failure to acknowledge our character issues and take deliberate time and effort to address those issues is one of the most common reasons that God may extend our time on the plateau.

Character issues will sometimes reveal themselves through a person's attitudes, temperament, disposition and moral fiber. These can quickly undermine and erode the ground that person is standing on. These vulnerabilities will slowly start to chip away at the person's credibility. If, for example, someone is manipulative and he has a tendency to lie in order to bend people to his will, his character will eventually be suspect, and the people associated with him will no longer be able to trust him. No one likes being lied to or manipulated. Regretfully, character issues will often keep an individual stuck in one place much longer than necessary.

At Inspire Church, we have just been through the most important season of transition that we have ever experienced. In any growing organization, change and transition have to be a proactive part of their DNA if they are going to adapt to the ongoing changes in the community and the world around them. There will also be events and circumstances that emerge suddenly and unexpectedly, such as a natural disaster, a riot or terrorist attack, or economic crisis that everyone must be prepared to address at a moment's notice. If you have a culture that is proactive, you can avoid being reactionary when these circumstances arise suddenly.

In order to care for our rapidly growing and geographically dispersed congregation more effectively, we reorganized our entire staff structure around a regional pastor model. We were blessed to have a model to adopt from a church in New Zealand called Life. Pastors Paul and Maree DeJong were so gracious in helping us to apply this model of ministry care into our own context. This initially involved moving 7 to 9 staff members from their ministry positions to a whole new different alignment of positions and priorities: seven regional pastors, a regional supervisor, and a regional administrator. We hired new staff and shifted current staff members to take on the ministry responsibilities that were previously assigned to our new regional pastors. When the process was complete, nearly 80% of the church staff had undergone a shift in their ministry responsibilities and assignments.

During this transition, we found it necessary to prune back some of our staff in order to continue to journey with those who truly owned our heart and vision for Inspire Church. Not everyone can stomach the change that happens to get you off a plateau. These adjustments on the apex of the curve were critical for us to care for every member of Inspire that wanted to be cared for. These changes can prove to be the most difficult and were a real test of my own character and leadership.

When pressure increases, what is in your heart will spill out. Our actions and words reveal what has been hiding on the inside. If bitterness and anger surface during these times, it's because the bitterness and anger were already there, lying dormant and ready to rise to the surface. True character will reveal itself in pressurized environments. When the heat is turned up, we often rip off our masks and our true colors will show for all to see. If you are a leader, you may no longer just be dealing with someone's changed assignment in a new season, you may find yourself having to face inappropriate emotions, attitudes and character issues that will need to be addressed and adjusted.

Most people don't like change, and many people resist change, or try to avoid it altogether. We have a saying at our church, "Blessed are the flexible, for they will not be bent out of shape."

One of our core values is, "We are not built to last; we are built to change." When you are built to last, defensive phrases like "Why the change?" or, "It was working fine, so why do we need to fix it?" are often used during plateaus. You may not be in charge of the circumstances surrounding your plateau, but you can be the master of your own emotions as you work toward preparing to move forward and upward.

> *Search me, O God, and know my heart; test me and know my anxious thoughts. Point out anything in me that offends you, and lead me along the path of everlasting life.*
>
> **Psalm 139:23-24 NLT**

Plateau seasons will reveal your character. Accelerate the process by inviting God to reveal any hidden character flaws that need to be dealt with. The Holy Spirit will often bring much to the surface that you were unaware of and shed light on many character and emotional issues that need to be addressed while you are on a plateau. A plateau provides an excellent opportunity for you and I to address the issues in our hearts. Don't try to go it alone. Be sure to partner with the Holy Spirit to refine your character. It's actually part of his job description:

But the Holy Spirit produces this kind of fruit in our lives: love, joy, peace, patience, kindness, goodness, faithfulness, gentleness, and self-control. There is no law against these things! Those who belong to Christ Jesus have nailed the passions and desires of their sinful nature to his cross and crucified them there. Since we are living by the Spirit, let us follow the Spirit's leading in every part of our lives.

Galatians 5:22-25

Plateaus are times when previous titles, positions and honors may no longer be relevant are are often stripped away at worst or changed at best. The Lord uses this as an opportunity for you to rediscover and redefine who you are at the core of our being and reflect on your primary life purpose and mission. Have you ever thought that maybe God wants to redefine who you are? Is your past identity holding you back and preventing Him from accomplishing all that He wants to in your life? My identity was wrapped up in my MLM. It was how people knew me and looking back, I discovered how important that was to me. When I left our sending church to be the new senior pastor of Inspire, it took over a year for me to finally let go of my old youth ministry because I didn't realize how much I loved it and how much I found my identity in it. I grieved for that period of time as I found out that I actually loved leading a church. Now the new challenge was to be defined more on the basis of *who I am in Jesus versus what I do for Him*. I'll have more time to elaborate on this in the last part of this book.

If you're leading a business or church through a season of significant change or working your way through a plateau, there is always an inherent danger of character issues surfacing in your own life. If you do not address these with humility and grace, there is a danger that your team members can be affected and potentially damaged by your character flaws acting out.

The same is true for your staff members. On several occasions, I have observed staff members who were either demoted or released from the team because of character issues. Those very issues that got them into trouble in the first place proved to be just the tip of the iceberg. When a person moves into crisis mode and is trying to do damage control, they often take their issues to social media and to their circles of influence to tell their side of the story. This can lead others to become disillusioned with the leadership if they are not wise and mature enough to recognize that there is always more than one side to a story.

You can either tackle the problem head-on, or you can choose not to address it and let it go. If you let it ride, it will come back to bite you. You've heard it said before, "Hurting people, hurt people." It is so true. If you're on a plateau and discouragement sets in, and if you recognize that you are one of these people who tends to spread your grievances around, it is time to work on your own character. Take it to the Lord and invite Him to scrub your heart.

Do not allow your character flaws to remain uncorrected, or you will remain on your plateau until you have grown and learned these lessons well.

3. Resistance to Change

Any person, church or business is going to need to change in this increasingly fast-paced, fast-changing world. I look back at all the changes just in technology alone, and it's enough to keep your head spinning. When the first commercially produced manual type-writer was introduced in the 1860s, it took another 80 to 90 years until the electronic typewriter was the number one office tool used besides the telephone. Just two decades later in the early 1980s the first desktop computers and word-processors were introduced, but it was almost 10 years before they replaced typewriters in most of-fices and schools.

We now live in an age where smart phones and tablets can perform most of the functions that desktop computers were designed to do. The models in each brand are upgraded every six months, quickly making older phones and tablets obsolete. New applications or "apps" for these phones are developed daily and upgrades for some of these apps come out weekly. Bottom line, we live in an age where the technology we use on a daily basis is changing faster than at any other time in history.

We live in an age when we cannot afford to be content to stay the same. In his book *Good to Great*, author Jim Collins essentially brakes it down and says, "few companies become great simply because it's just so easy to settle for good." I would add to that paraphrase by saying that it's not just that we are satisfied with good, but that we are afraid of the challenges and hard work that come along with the change that precedes the success you desire. If you choose to stay resistant to change, you will become stuck on a plateau; and if you are already on a plateau, you will remain on it much longer than originally needed.

When change is encountered or introduced, ask yourself this question: "Is the Lord behind this change?" If He is, be quick to embrace it. If God is not necessarily behind the change, ask if the change is compatible with the direction and purpose that God has given you to follow. If you recognize that it is compatible, seek His guidance regarding how to best leverage the change to accomplish His purposes. If you wrestle with being the initiator of change even when God has guided you to make the change, then you need to learn to trust that God will use this change for your good, and the good of your church, business or organization.

In the book of Genesis, Joseph did not ask to be sold into slavery by his brothers, but he was. It was beyond his control. Joseph went from the slave caravan to work in Potiphar's home. Potiphar was the captain of Pharaoh's bodyguard. Joseph was falsely accused of attempting to rape Potiphar's wife and was sent to prison. He languished in prison for over two years. None of these changes were pleasant or even Joseph's fault, yet he never despaired. He held onto the dreams that God had given him back in his Father's home. So wherever Joseph ended up, he worked as though he was working for the Lord, and through each season he found favor in the eyes of his superiors and was promoted to a high level of leadership and responsibility. His circumstances could have been depressing, but Joseph continued to find favor with God.

Throughout his plateau, Joseph pressed in to God and continued to mature in wisdom and character as he continued to develop the skills he would need one day as the Vizier of Egypt. After a season, the Pharaoh himself recognized Joseph's wisdom, skills and character, and instantly, Joseph was promoted from the depths of the prison to the heights of Pharaoh's palace. All of us would be wise to follow Joseph's example to cooperate with God to utilize our changing times and situations as opportunities to be transformed for the better. You can either fight the change and possibly find yourself unemployed, or you can embrace the change, guard your heart, and allow God to bring promotion in His timing.

4. The Orphan Mindset

The 'orphan spirit' or 'orphan mindset' refers to a spiritual condition in which a Christian is able to outwardly profess to know God as Father; however, there are deep internal struggles with feelings of rejection, abandonment, inadequacy, and neglect, and an overall "victim" mindset. An orphan spirit is often due to unhealed hurts from painful past experiences with authority figures, especially their parents. An orphan spirit can go undetected, until circumstances, such as fast-paced change, cause the individual's insecurity and anxiety to surface. Some ways that an 'orphan spirit' can manifest in team members include: fear and distrust for those in authority, insecure feelings about their position or title, a need to prove their worth, throw adult forms of tantrums in a passive aggressive manner, are in constant need for approval and attention, etc… They are like a child that's been adopted into a family that cares and feeds them well every day, but secretly hides food under the bed for fear of never having enough to eat or another meal again. They gather as much as they can but rarely give all of themselves. Left unchecked, this mindset and can cause great damage to a team and often derails them of their destiny. Unless lessons are learned and great breakthrough happens, they will remain on a plateau for long seasons unless they choose to break away for another location or another situation but finds themselves repeating the same cycle.

But on the positive side, if it is apparent that this person is willing to submit themselves to a healthy process (professional counseling, prayer), there can be incredible freedom and undying loyalty. People in these predicaments require extra grace and love because at the root of it all is a need for approval and acceptance.

5. Spiritual Warfare

God advances His kingdom through the growth He brings about in your own life and in your family, in your business or ministry, and in all of the people your life touches throughout the week. The enemy is severely threatened whenever the Kingdom of God is advancing so he actively opposes all development and advancement in your life, and he attempts to prevent your progress from positively impacting those around you. As a result, during times of change, transition, and the growth that transpires, your personal and family life, your business, your church or ministry, indeed every aspect of your life, can become a prime target for spiritual attack.

An example of this can be seen in the book of Nehemiah. Nehemiah was the former cupbearer of Artaxerxes I, King of Persia. Nehemiah was sent to Judah by King Artaxerxes to serve as territorial governor to oversee the reconstruction of Jerusalem's walls. Throughout the entire project to rebuild the walls, the enemies of Judah were trying to distract and intimidate Nehemiah and attack the workers on the wall to bring the project to a halt. Like Nehemiah, we need to be aware of how the enemy works in order to circumvent his strategy and foil his attacks so we that we will be able to move forward to complete the work that God has given us to do.

> *Be strong in the Lord and in his mighty power. Put on all of God's armor so that you will be able to stand firm against all strategies of the devil. For we are not fighting against flesh-and-blood enemies, but against evil rulers and authorities of the unseen world, against mighty powers in this dark world, and against evil spirits in the heavenly places. Therefore, put on every piece of God's armor so you will be able to resist the enemy in the time of evil. Then after the battle you will still be standing firm.* **Ephesians 6:10-13 NLT**

When spiritual warfare is coming at a ministry from the outside, it can be relatively easy to detect and identify the source so you will be able to counter it. Sometimes, however, the most potent spiritual warfare is internal, stirring within a team.

> *Stay alert! Watch out for your great enemy, the devil. He prowls around like a roaring **lion**, looking for someone to devour.* **1 Peter 5:8**

Like a lion stalking his prey, the enemy works by seeking out the most vulnerable members in a group: the weakest, the youngest, the wounded or the isolated. He seeks out those struggling in any of the above four areas we have just discussed: those struggling with discouragement, those with character flaws and immaturity, those resistant to change, and those who feel like orphans. He targets their weaknesses and aggravates them in order to distract and disable the team member, or even take them out of the game. He will then harness their weaknesses to divide, and if possible, destroy the team.

> *'Do not let the sun go down while you are still angry, and do not give the devil a foothold.'* **(Ephesians 4:26-27)**

As soon as they are recognized, it is vital that hurts and offences be addressed immediately and not allowed to fester. Those who operate out of a divisive spirit are often those who have unhealed hurts or unfulfilled expectations from the past or present that have not been dealt with. The best way to take care of the spiritual warfare at work within a team is to prevent it before the enemy is able to infiltrate the hearts of any of the team members.

- Be pro-active.
- Be intentional and strategic to head off any potential areas of vulnerability before they become pronounced enough to be noticed.
- Develop a culture of honor.
- Foster team unity.
- Encourage and affirm those struggling with discouragement.
- Help each team member grow past any identified character flaws and immaturity.
- Coach those resistant to change on how to harness the positive aspects of change to their benefit.
- Create a family atmosphere of love and inclusion, where each member is valued for who they are and what they contribute to the team, so that no one feels like an orphan or an outcast.

Forewarned is forearmed, so teach your team members to recognize the strategies and tactics of the enemy in advance of the attacks. Develop their sense of spiritual discernment and heighten their alertness to changes in the environment around them that may be due to the influence of the enemy. Help them learn to identify the signs that demonic attack may be occurring during a significant time of transition or change. Train them to utilize the skills of a spiritual warrior. Teach them to properly outfit themselves with the armor of God. Equip them to wield the mighty weapons at their disposal to fend off the attack of the enemy and send him fleeing in retreat.

> *Therefore, **put on every piece of God's armor** so you will be able to resist the enemy in the time of evil. Then after the battle you will still be standing firm.*
>
> *Ephesians 6:13-18 NLT*

- *Stand your ground, putting on the **belt of truth***
- *and the **body armor of God's righteousness.***
- ***For shoes, put on the peace that comes from the Good News** so that you will be fully prepared.*
- *In addition to all of these, hold up the **shield of faith** to stop the fiery arrows of the devil.*
- *Put on **salvation as your helmet,***
- *and take **the sword of the Spirit, which is the word of God.***
- ***Pray in the Spirit** at all times and on every occasion.*
- ***Stay alert and be persistent in your prayers for all believers everywhere.***

Prepare them to stand guard, supporting each other and those in leadership. Disarm the enemy by healing hurts and resolving offenses in an upfront and healthy manner. Maintain the team's worship and corporate prayer life to maintain team health and foster *esprit du corps*. Don't allow the busyness that accompanies change to weaken the quality of the spiritual life of individual team members and the team as a whole. Also make sure that every team member gets adequate rest, good nutrition, and ample exercise or recreation so that fatigue, illness and stress do not make them more vulnerable to the enemy's attack.

By remaining alert and diligent, we will do well to prepare ourselves for a new season. Honoring God and honoring the process will set you up for the next phase of your journey. But God's discernment and wisdom will serve you well to make sure that what you are to embark on, as my good friend John Bevere says is it "Good or God?"

CHAPTER ELEVEN

IS YOUR NEW "PEAK" REALLY A PEAK?

Sometimes when you are on a plateau, the very best thing you can do is to stay right where you are and dig in. Be diligent to partner with God to accomplish His purposes for you while you are on your plateau. Some important questions that you need to ask yourself are:

- Am I jumping from one plateau situation to another?
- Am I trying to trade the situation God has me in for a situation of my own choosing?
- Am I inadvertently circumventing God's character formation and the refining process that He intended for me to undergo while on my plateau?

When things seem to be going well for you, it's easier to remain in one place. When you've hit a personal or professional plateau, not every plateau is a crisis. In fact, most plateaus are relatively benign.

There may be delays in moving forward, but it is not necessarily unpleasant in your current location. When you are on a plateau, things are relatively stable and you are not facing a lot of new challenges, so there is a far smaller drain on your mental, emotional, spiritual and energy resources. This can afford you the mental, spiritual and emotional flexibility, as well as the surplus time and energy needed to deal with any lingering issues from your past that will help prepare you well for the next stage of your life journey.

Sure, there are going to be times when God is leading you to leave your current situation. Under the best circumstances, there will be a sense of call to a new vocation or a new type of ministry. Before you consider making a change, make sure you are hearing God's call and you are not just seeking an easy escape from your plateau. If you are seriously contemplating such a move, take some personal leave or vacation time to remove yourself from your situation temporarily so you will have greater clarity to discern God's call. Then you can make your move with the confidence that God is leading the way. But one thing to really keep in mind is that "the way you exit is the way you enter." In other words, if you leave well, you will enter your new season with honor and a clean conscience. If you left poorly, were unappreciative or "talked trash" out the door or even months later, you have sown seed into your new environment that will eventually bear fruit.

If you leave your current plateau just because you are discontent, disappointed, or bored in your current situation, you may regret the decision you made. Changing one plateau for what seems to be greener pastures can actually backfire on you. Why? Because in doing so, we end up circumventing and short-circuiting the character-building process that God may have intended for you on your plateau. In order to be properly prepared to climb again, God will need to fashion a new crucible to purify your heart and your character to replace the one you removed yourself from prematurely. Then you may need to begin the process all over again.

Look around you. Is the environment around you healthy? Are the people you're working with good people with integrity of character? If so, then it may be possible that you are the unhealthy one bringing the drama to your team and coworkers. If you are the primary source of the problem, or even if you're just a part of the problem, then jumping from one plateau to what seems to be a better situation will only transplant your issues into a new situation. This is never the wise thing to do at this juncture. The best thing that you can do is to stay right where you are. Learn the lessons that you need to learn, that God intends for you to learn, and make the most of managing the middle. You can change your environment and surroundings but if you haven't changed then your taking the same person (you) and the same situation (your challenges) are just taking them to a new location and it *will* resurface *unless* you…change.

There is a time when it is beneficial to jump off your plateau and seek another. That time is when your situation and the atmosphere around you are toxic and corrosive. The very life is being sucked out of you, and you are being crushed by the weight of the circumstances and people around you. There may be times when God tells you to pack your bags and flee, like Lot and his family, before the fire and brimstone start falling. Even under these conditions, it is best to make sure you are actually hearing God's command to get out now and not just hearing your inner voice over-reacting to the challenges and difficulties of going through major change or transition. There may also be times when God calls you to take the spiritual offensive to reclaim the toxic situation for God. If so, be sure that the Holy Spirit is leading the charge so that you're not setting out to slay the dragon all on your own.

Successful managing the middle will afford you the opportunity to master your emotions. Milk your plateau for all the character development it's worth to get every last drop into your heart. Leverage your time on the plateau to identify the stumbling blocks to your growth and remove them. If you feel that you need it, get some professional counseling to help you overcome stubborn emotional issues and pursue inner healing. Most importantly, seek God like you've never sought him before. God isn't just to be found on the glory of the mountaintop. Like Jesus during his earthly ministry, God chooses to hang out with the broken, the outcasts, the sick and the suffering, the sinners, the seekers and the strugglers. He is right there with you on your plateau. You only have to reach out to Him, and He will meet you right where you are.

The story of Abraham, Ishmael and Isaac, the son of the promise and the work of the flesh, provides a powerful example of what happens when you try to shorten your stay on the plateau that God has placed you on by seeking out another seemingly shorter plateau. All plateaus look smaller than they actually are when they are viewed from a distance.

When Abraham was 75 years old, God promised him that he would be the father of a great nation. Although God repeated His promise to Abraham several years after He made that initial promise, several more years passed and Abraham still had no son of his own. When he was 85 years old, and his wife Sarah was 75 years old and still barren, she was now decades beyond being able to conceive and carry a child naturally. Abraham had waited ten long years for God to make good on His promise.

During the time of Abraham and in his native culture, it was acceptable and legally valid for a woman to bear children by proxy through her female servant. So Sarah offered her servant Hagar to Abraham to conceive a child in her name. Sarah reasoned that God had not made any move toward fulfilling His promise, so Abraham may have reasoned that God must be expecting him to make accommodations to provide an heir who will carry on his lineage and produce the great nation God had promised. Abraham slept with Hagar and nine months later, Ishmael was born.

What Abraham and Sarah reasoned was the best solution for their ongoing plateau was definitely not God's solution. Unless God is leading you off of your plateau, you can't successfully trade in your plateau for another, even when it seems to be the reasonable and even culturally acceptable thing to do. If you are ever going to move forward onto the heights of God's promise, be very sure that it's HIS way or no way at all.

The folly of their decision became evident even before Ishmael was born. Hagar became prideful and arrogant, flaunting her easy pregnancy before Sarah. At the same time, Hagar tried to win 86-year-old Abraham's favor and affection as he expectantly awaited the birth of his first child. Sarah, in turn, treated Hagar abusively and drove her out of the camp. What was supposed to bring a blessing, instead brought tension and conflict into Abraham's household even before Ishmael was born.

Everything only became more complicated after Ishmael was born. Abraham was thrilled to have a son from his own loins as his heir, and he took great delight in his son, but Sarah was miserable. Hagar became even more prideful and competitive with Sarah, rubbing her face in the fact that Hagar had been able to give Abraham a son, and Sarah remained childless. When Abraham and Sarah took things into their own hands and tried to get off their plateau of waiting for the fulfillment of God's promise, they not only created much discord in their family, they probably delayed even further, God's intent to give Sarah a child through a miraculous conception, pregnancy and childbirth.

Abraham jumped from one prolonged plateau of delay to another even longer and more complicated plateau. They waited an additional thirteen years before God once again reaffirmed His original covenant with Abraham. Abraham was now 99 and Sarah was 89 years old. God clearly told Abraham and Sarah that it had been His intent all along to provide them with their son of promise through

Sarah. Miraculously, 89-year-old Sarah conceived and gave birth to their son within the year. God also promised to extend a portion of Abraham's blessing to Ishmael, but He now also required that all males in Abraham's household and all of his male descendants from that time forward were to be circumcised.

Abraham was 100 years old and Sarah was 90 when their long-awaited son of promise was finally born. Isaac's birth did not resolve all of the issues created when Abraham tried to fulfill God's promise on his own. Though Ishmael still had much affection from Abraham as his firstborn, he became jealous of Isaac. On the day of Isaac's weaning celebration, Sarah caught Ishmael abusing Isaac, and she demanded that Abraham send Hagar and Ishmael away permanently. Sarah did not want Ishmael to share in Isaac's inheritance, nor did she want Ishmael to be able to harm Isaac ever again.

Ishmael and Isaac were both from Abraham's seed. One was the result of a natural conception and childbirth, the other the result of a supernatural conception and miraculous childbirth. One was the child of compromise, the second the child of promise. Both would become fathers of great nations, but the covenant with Yahweh would only be given to Isaac.

When your sojourn on your plateau grows long and the end is nowhere in sight, beware of taking things into your own hands to try to bring your plateau to a premature end. Stay the course. God is faithful and He will always make good on His promises. Don't end up trading in the divine promise of your Isaac, for the human solution of an Ishmael. The world is still paying the consequences of Abraham's one poor decision to shortcut his plateau.

Be wise! Continue to wait faithfully upon God's promise on the plateau He has for you right now. Don't circumvent the refining processes of God's character formation in your life. God intends to forge the character of Christ in you while you are on your plateau, so don't try to rush the process. Stay right where you are and dig in. Don't be sidetracked when you see others who are prospering after moving on from their plateau. Don't be tempted to force the issue by taking things into your own hands. Rather, be diligent to partner with God to accomplish His purposes for you while you wait on your plateau.

> **Be still** before the LORD, and **wait** patiently for him;
> **do not fret** over those who prosper in their way,
> over those who carry out evil devices.   **Psalm 37:7**

> I **wait** for the LORD, my soul **waits**,
> and **in his word I hope**;
> my soul **waits for the Lord**
> more than those who watch for the morning,
> more than those who watch for the morning.   **Psalm 130:5-6**

Edited through this point, the remainder should become part of a third section on preparing for your ascent.

Part Three

Getting Ready for Your Next Mountain Peak

CHAPTER TWELVE

THE "RE"-ALITIES OF VALLEYS

As I mentioned earlier in this book, valleys are great places to be. You can't avoid the valley, unless of course, you want to remain on your plateau. Since you've read all the way through to this point, I'm assuming that if you're on a plateau or if you ever get there, you will eventually want to get off that plateau and head toward the next peak.

However, life isn't just about the mountaintops. There are valleys and plateaus in between those summits. And just as the plateaus in life are inevitable, so are the valleys. Valleys can be two things. First of all, they can be *difficult*. As I pointed out in Part Two, a lot of people describe the downturns on life's timeline as trials and tribulation. I completely understand that. Many of the challenges have already been addressed in the previous two sections of this book. But there is one more challenge that I would like to prepare you for, and that is the first "Re" of the **Realities: Re**sistance.

RESISTANCE

Although **re**sistance is a familiar challenge to many, it still remains puzzling to some. In fact, I am often amazed that people are surprised when they encounter **re**sistance. **Re**sistance is as old as the Garden of Eden. Even before the Garden, the Devil had been actively **re**sisting God himself. So we shouldn't be surprised when we encounter opposition and **re**sistance as soon as we are motivated to get off our plateaus and begin to climb again. Opposition and **re**sistance will often cause people to avoid trying to go to the "next level" for fear that they will be overcome. But if you want to do anything great for God, you have to expect **re**sistance.

Gravity is a common example of physical **re**sistance. We all know it exists. Although we may have first learned to call it "gravity" in an elementary science class, we have all experienced gravity since the day we attempted to take our first head-wobbling, big-eyed steps. Though we stumbled at first, it did not prevent us from eventually being able to walk. Gravity is always present, but we rarely think about it.

Even if I were to think about gravity, it wouldn't stop me from jumping or even surfing. I don't yell at the golf ball for landing on the grass and yell, "Darn that Gravity! I'll show you!" No, gravity is just a part of life to be conscious of and to overcome. Just because I don't levitate and hover up to the mountain peak, it won't prevent me from continuing to climb. The same is true with **re**sistance and opposition. We need to be conscious of it, work to overcome it, and continue to move onward and upward.

Pastor Craig Groeschel leads one of America's largest churches, a church based in Oklahoma called Life.Church. As of this writing, they meet each week at 25 campuses in 7 states. With attendance ranging upward of 70,000 per weekend, Life.Church recently reached 100,000 people during the summer! (Who grows during the summer?) Craig recently preached at our church, sharing a message called "Bold Obedience." He challenged my heart as he spoke about opposition,

"I worry sometimes more when I'm not experiencing opposition because that may be an indicator that I'm not boldly obeying God. Boldly obeying God often triggers opposition. If you are not ready to face opposition for obeying God, you are not ready to be used by God."

Before you begin moving on to the next phase of your climb, it is wise for you to establish the fact that you will encounter opposition. The Devil isn't going to just roll out the red carpet for you. Neither is he just going to roll over. No, he's going to put up a fight and wage war against you and everything that God has called you to accomplish. There will be pushback. I'm not writing this to scare you, I'm just informing you of the reality. Even if you already know this, it's good to be reminded that you will face resistance from the enemy as you obediently work to advance Christ's kingdom here on earth. In fact, to take a different angle on Craig's quote, be encouraged when you face resistance and opposition, it means that you are making significant headway for Christ's kingdom, and the enemy feels very threatened.

Plateaus can be difficult. Secondly, plateaus and valleys can also be *developmental*. The valley is where you'll discover incredible gems that will develop you for that next mountain peak. I call these gems the "**Re**"-alities of the valleys.

REKINDLE

As you head toward the next valley, preparation is key. The first and most important objective in your planning is prayer. Fully immerse yourself and every leg of your journey in prayer. **Re**kindle the passion of your love for God; seek His face as you've never sought Him before. As you pursue Him, you'll **re**discover your God-given purpose and potential once again. God will **re**veal stunning vistas and inspirational horizons that He has already prepared for you. Draw closer to the Lord than you've ever been before. Draw so close to Him that you'll be able to see things with the same heart and perspective as God himself.

How do I know this? From time to time, I have inadvertently tried to do it all on my own – without seeking God first. I never meant to go it alone, but there have been a few brief seasons in my life when I neglected my daily time of prayer and reading God's Word. I came up with what I thought were great ideas, but those ideas were just Mike-ideas rather than God-breathed inspirations. My plans weren't rooted and grounded and filled to overflowing with the full intent and blessing of God's heart, mind and spirit.

I know. I should've known better. But before you judge me, I'll bet you've made the same mistakes too. There's no excuse for it, but I just... got... "busy." Without an intentional, committed daily time with God, I found myself getting a little burned out and a just a little bit "crispy" around the edges, as my friends and I like to say. I needed to slow myself down. I needed to be deliberate: to purposefully reserve a part of each day to rekindle my passion for God, to redirect my focus toward Him, and to reacquaint myself with Jesus once again.

One of my favorite passages in the Bible is found in the book of Psalms. In Psalm 37:3-4 David writes,

> *Trust in the LORD AND DO GOOD.*
> *Then you will live safely in the land and prosper.*
> **Take delight in the LORD,**
> **and he will give you your heart's desires.**
> *Commit everything you do to the LORD.*
> *Trust him, and he will help you.*   *(NLT)*

When we **rekindle** our passion for God and we **re**commit our lives fully and completely to Him, we begin to live the life that He has planned and purposed for us. We live a life invested in His Kingdom – for His purposes, and for His glory – and God begins to give you the desires of your heart. He gives you Himself! All of the things that you've been concerned about…all "these things" begin to fall into place and take its correct order in your life. Let me put this another way. Our lists start to **re**prioritize themselves in the presence of the Lord.

In Jesus's day, the people were just as concerned about the very same things that we are concerned about today. The everyday trials, issues and concerns that mattered most to them are the same trials, issues and concerns that we face right here today. Knowing their hearts were worried and troubled, and seeing that they were like sheep without a shepherd and without spiritual purpose, Jesus said to them:

> *But seek first his kingdom and his righteousness, and all these things will be given to you as well.*
>
> **Matthew 6:33 NLT**

Something amazing began to happen as I chose to seek God above all else, even as I struggled alone on a plateau a long time ago. It was during that season that I found myself wrestling between what I felt I was called to do as opposed to what I truly wanted for myself. There was a tug-of-war being fought in my heart. I was a double-minded man, just like the one the apostle James describes in James 1:6-8,

> *But when you ask Him (for wisdom), be sure that your faith is in God alone. Do not waver, for a person with divided loyalty is as unsettled as a wave of the sea that is blown and tossed by the wind. Such people should not expect to receive anything from the Lord. Their loyalty is divided between God and the world, and they are unstable in everything they do.* **James 1:6-8 NLT**

So I decided that I would *"delight myself in the Lord,"* just like Psalm 37:3-4 said, and I made the Kingdom of God my primary concern. I remember asking Him, "Lord, does this glorify you?"

At that time, I understood the phrase, "delighting myself in the LORD," in the same light and in the same ways that I would "delight myself" in Lisa back when we were dating... back when dinosaurs roamed the earth... back when people actually wrote letters to each other, Lisa and I treasured exchanging letters. Since I was a single parent working long hours while caring for my young daughter, I wasn't able to see Lisa on a regular basis. Most of our courtship took place over the phone and through the occasional letter. Although we lived only fifteen minutes away from each other, we took the deliberate time to record on paper our special thoughts, plans and dreams to each another.

I loved when Lisa wrote to me because back then; she would express herself on paper more clearly than when we talked face-to-face. Before she mailed each letter to me, she would spray a little of her perfume on the paper so that when I opened the envelope, I would know that my "one and only" was thinking of me. After I read each letter, I would sigh a long, deep sigh... then inhale deeply the scent of her perfume on the note... and hold her precious words close to my heart for a long time. Yes, I was and still am a hopeless romantic.

My love for Lisa and the pure delight of pursuing my relationship with my beloved caused me to approach my time of delighting myself in the Lord in much the same way. Within a few months, a funny thing happened. As I began delighting myself in the Lord – praying daily, reading my Bible, and seeking after Him like never before, my desires began to change. At first, I thought that the Lord had tricked me, but I soon realized what really happened. I had begun to want only what God wanted for me. Soon, His desires (God's plans and purposes for me) became the ultimate desires of my heart. All I wanted was what He wanted.

160

REFRESH

One way that we can **re**fresh ourselves in the valleys is to give ourselves time to enjoy activities outside of our regular, everyday work lives. We all need to be able to pursue those interests and activities that will help us **re**-discover and **re**-create our lives through our interests, gifts and talents. These may be hobbies that we may have long neglected, new interests that we have wanted to explore, developing skills and techniques in a specific activity or sport, or the challenge of acquiring more knowledge and experience in areas other than our current vocation.

For me, my opportunity to **re**fresh myself was a project to build a table. Just prior to my last two-month sabbatical to rest and **re**calibrate myself, I started to build a table. Please understand that I am not much of a handyman, but I am able fix to a few things around the house. I love working hard any time a home improvement project calls for me to hire someone. I've been able to help remodel our home as an "assistant" to the carpenters, built a redwood fence around my home, as well as other things that I'm honestly quite proud of.

Lisa shared with me her dream for our family dinners. She wanted a dining table large enough to accommodate our whole family. Lisa and I love our kids. We have been blessed with an ever-growing family that now includes our very first grandchild, a beautiful, bright-eyed little girl named Bowie.

When the time came to start my project, I did what any bright, skilled, industrious, modern man would do today. I looked it up on Pinterest! I looked at and considered all kinds of plans, decided on the table that would be the perfect one for our family, then **re**cruited my son-in-law, Jaysen, and my close friend, Rob to help me build it. By the time summer was almost over, I'd become an expert at building tables! As a matter of fact, when I finished our sturdy, brand new, one-of-a-kind, handcrafted, farmhouse table for eight, my friend who is a dealer in fine exotic woods told me that I would probably be able to sell our table for over $4,000!

This table did more than just deliver a beautiful gift to my wife on Thanksgiving Day. Some day it will become a precious heirloom passed down to one of my daughters (whoever is nicest to me and promises to take care of me in my old age). In the process of building the table, I learned that just by reading through the instructions carefully and completely, and then diligently applying myself to the task, I could accomplish a lot.

In ministry, most of the work we do always seems to be unfinished. People's lives are always "in process" along their life journey, and "Inspiring people to fulfill their God-given potential" never ceases. On the other hand, as I continued to work on the table a little more each day, I had the unique opportunity to see the results of my labor at the end of each day, and I had the satisfaction of experiencing the entire building process from beginning to end.

The table project also gave me a chance to take my mind off of the pressures and stresses of everyday life and work, and allowed me to refocus on learning and developing a brand new skill. Refresh yourself in new ways for each new season. Rediscover some old pursuits that need to have a place in your life once again.

REINVEST

Valleys are gathering places. Pour your life into the lives of others. The valley is not all about you.

> *Whoever finds his life will lose it, and whoever loses his life for my sake will find it.* **Matthew 10:39 ESV**

In Matthew 10, Jesus was teaching His disciples and followers about living a totally new, totally transformed life. He was adamant that they would truly know and fully comprehend this brand new way of thinking and living; they would realize that this was about giving up everything they knew and valued in order to truly be His disciples and follow Him. In every way possible, Jesus was determined to help His followers recognize that their brand new Kingdom life in Him was in total contrast to the familiar worldly life they were accustomed to living.

In verse 39, Jesus explained that when one chooses to follow Him, they would need to be prepared to completely surrender their life in order to follow Him. Essentially, Jesus was asking His followers to "count the cost." If they chose to follow Him, they could be martyred. And many of them were. Even those who did not have to face martyrdom gave up their present lives and everything they held near and dear to their hearts.

He told them that when you choose to give up your life, you will find your life – the life you always wanted and needed – but just never really knew how or where to look. When you take your eyes off yourself and refocus your heart on serving others for the sake of God's Kingdom, you will begin to find the new, real life you've always wanted and desired deep down in your heart.

When I finally gave in and surrendered my whole heart to God, He gave me His amazing love. When I gave Him all of the life goals and ambitions I'd established for myself, He gave me a whole brand new life that I had never dreamed I would actually be living!

Today, you often hear people say that they are "Living the dream!" Well, when God calls you to let go, He will always replace it with something even better. For those who are willing to let go in obedience to the Lord, you will have that new life, and you will live a life that you never thought was possible. He's not promising you a vacation home in the Hamptons or even in Hawaii. He's not promising to give you all of your heart's desires. But! What He is promising you is His best for you. After all, isn't that the life we want to live…the life He desires to give us?

Jesus said, "I have come that they may have life and have it to the full."   **John 10:10 NIV**

No matter where we are or what's happening in our lives, the Holy Spirit says through the Apostle Paul,

"... I have learned to live with much and learned to live with little... I can do all things through Christ who strengthens me."   **Philippians 4:12-13**

What God did for Paul, He can also do for you and me.

REINVENT

One of the great advantages of heading into the valley is that a valley is a great environment in which to reinvent ourselves. Just recently, I have come off of a different plateau. I am passionate about basketball. I have been playing the sport since I was a little boy and have been playing it at a very competitive level even into my forties. Until recently, I had planned to play into my sixties! Why? Because I have seen some incredible men in that age range play at a high enough level that even the *young guns* in their 20's had to work to keep up. It's something I really enjoy, and it is my chosen form of exercise.

As a side note, a few years ago John Bevere introduced me to the game of golf. Now you have to understand that I never thought of golf as a sport that required any level of athletic prowess. I used to say to myself, *how ridiculous is this? Hitting a little white ball into a hole?* John once told me, "Mike, one of the main reasons pastors stumble in their race is because they don't have a hobby." I replied, "John, I play basketball 2 to 3 times a week and I'm going to play until I'm a very old man." To which John said, "Mike, there may come a time that you can't run as hard and jump as high as you would like, so you might as well learn golf now before you get too to old to be good at it." Finally, I relented and took him up on his offer. I live in Hawaii and we are known for having some of the world's most beautiful golf courses, it made sense for me to learn the game. Although I hadn't quit playing basketball, John gave me my first set of starter golf clubs. I took some lessons and decided I should learn the game. The first thing I learned, is that nothing can humble you faster than the game of golf, it is much harder than I imagined! But, I've been playing the game ever since, and have grown to love it.

Then, it happened. During a game of pick-up basketball, I hyperextended my right knee. I noticed a strange feeling, but ignored it and kept playing. Then, two days later, I began to notice some significant swelling. I eventually had an MRI done and sat down with my orthopedic surgeon Dr. Darryl Kan, who is regarded as one of the top orthopedic surgeons in Hawaii. The news was not good. I had a torn meniscus in my right knee. In other words, I tore my cartilage and it would require surgery. This was quite a shock. You have to understand that I have never had an injury like this before. If fact, I had recently set a goal to dunk a basketball once again as I had in my youth. That might sound crazy or even borderline prideful, but I was determined. But now, in one brief moment, it was over. I was crushed, I *love* basketball! If I had to prioritize the the things in life that I love, I would say I love Jesus, my family, our church, and then… basketball.

Fast forward a few months, the surgery was successful. I was in and out of surgery and the recovery room in four hours. A friend of mine drove me home where I promptly elevated my knee and began to watch college basketball's premier yearly event, the NCAA Basketball Tournament, affectionately known as *March Madness* (thank you, Jesus!). On doctor's orders, I was not to apply any pressure on my knee for an entire week unless it was absolutely necessary. I could walk to the bathroom, to my bedroom, the kitchen and the couch to watch sports, but that was it. And I thoroughly enjoyed my recovery time as I watched every game that ESPN or

ABC Sports had scheduled. I was in heaven! Almost. But all of this just masked the reality that I would have to find new forms of exercise that would bring personal fulfillment, allow me some great fellowship with the same group of guys I have been playing with for five years, most of whom did not attend church at all. I enjoyed the physical contact of the game and the ability to satisfy the competitive side of my personality that was best manifested and expressed on the basketball court. The doctor told me that the recovery time and the possibly playing basketball again would be somewhere around six to nine months depending upon how my knee responded to the physical therapy. Both my physical therapist, who is married to my cousin, and Dr. Kan were very cautious in their estimation as to what level I would be able to play when I returned to the sport.

The reality of not playing Basketball was a difficult proposition. In addition to my love of the game, I was beginning to gain weight due to the lack of cardio exercise during recovery. Any form of exercise involving my legs was gone for the time being. I was in serious need of reinventing my existing form of exercise into a routine that involved the use of my upper body. When you exercise, your body releases chemicals called endorphins. These endorphins interact with the receptors in your brain that reduce your perception of pain and trigger a positive feeling in the body. For example, the feeling that follows a run or workout is often described as "euphoric." That feeling, known as a "runner's high," can be accompanied by an energizing outlook on life. The affect of physically exerting oneself has been also attributed to reducing stress and warding off feelings of depression and anxiety. Playing basketball did this for me. It kept me sane and allowed me to have an outlet to feel good about myself. When I am moving into an unusually busy time, I will purposely take the time to hit the gym for a workout or the courts for a quick game of pickup basketball. It was critical that I find a new outlet.

Hawaii is known for it's world-class golf and also it's many water sports, so I decided it was time to reinvent myself by choosing activities that would give me the needed exercise, but also the personal satisfaction and fellowship that basketball gave me. I made the decision to up my golf game, and also to find other sports that don't require the heavy use of my knees.

I called Philip, another cousin of mine, who lives on the beach in our area. Philip is regarded as one of the state's great watermen. Not only does he enjoy the stand-up paddle boards and canoes, he is an accomplished surfer and he even tow surfs (where men on Jet Skis "tow" surfers out onto huge, massive waves where paddling by hand would prove deadly (as if it wasn't treacherous enough). In fact, if there's a water sport that keeps you above the water, Philip has probably mastered it. He was more than happy to allow me to use his one-man canoe as he and I would paddle out to the Mokulua Islands just offshore from his home. I would get the strenuous exercise I needed and I would get to spend time on the water with Philip, who would pepper me with questions that ranged from theology to our family. I'm so thankful for him providing me the opportunity to join him in the warm waters of the Pacific Ocean, use his gear and clear my head. Although it doesn't compare to basketball, it sure comes in close when you factor in the beauty and the beach!

Although I may never compete in basketball at the level I used to before my injury, I'm sure going to give it my best shot. But if I never do, you won't find me feeling sorry for myself. What I have discovered about myself through this season is that I can adapt myself and reinvent alternative forms of exercise that I can get passionate about. I've learned to enjoy golfing, paddling and surfing.

Plateaus and valleys both call for periods of introspection. These are the times that we should be asking those closest to us what they think of us, and to share their observations of us in our daily lives. If you really want to know how others see you, make yourself vulnerable before them, and give them permission to be brutally honest.

It's easy for us to say that we want accountability, and we may even invite others to hold us accountable, but unless we're honest with everyone, and especially honest with ourselves, we are only play-acting (the Greek word for that is *hypocrites*) our way through the accountability process, and we end up only fooling ourselves. If we dare to be honest about who we truly are, if those who partner with us in the accountability process are willing to share the honest truth in love, and if we have the internal fortitude (guts) to receive it, great things can happen.

One of the benefits of the accountability process is that we get to reinvent ourselves before we begin our next season in life. You may not always be planning on reinventing yourself, but if you've been pressing in to God, it may be part of **His** plan for you.

Prior to becoming "Inspire Church," our church was known as "Hope Chapel West O`ahu." The very first "Hope Chapel" was planted by Pastor Ralph Moore in Hermosa Beach, California back in 1971. Since that time, "Hope Chapel" has grown into a movement of over 1500 churches worldwide. Hope Chapel churches come in various sizes, from house churches to mega churches. Not all of the churches that were started in this movement bear the same name, but since I'd been mentored personally by Pastor Ralph at Hope Chapel Kaneohe, we took the name Hope Chapel West O`ahu when we were sent out in 2001.

About eight years into our journey together, something unusual happened. The night before our "Equip and Inspire Conference," I had a dream that stayed with me as I woke up the next morning. After saying "I love you, Lisa" as I opened my eyes, and I thought to myself, "Man, how can I be so lucky," my heart flowed into a prayer of sincere gratitude, "Lord, thank you for blessing with such a beautiful wife!" The very next words out of my mouth were, "Babe, you are not going to believe the dream I had last night... I dreamt that we changed our church name!" My even-keeled, non-roller coaster riding wife said, "You're crazy! We are **not** doing that!"

"I know," I said.

I had too many other important things to worry about that morning. The *E & I Conference* was going to begin within the next few hours, and I still had to get dressed and head quickly over to the church as soon as I possibly could.

Then something very interesting happened. As I was greeting all of the guests streaming through our church doors, one of my closest friends, Pastor Fernando Castillo, came up to me and said, "Bro, you are not going to believe what happened in the parking lot!" I asked him to tell me about it and he said, "When I was walking to your building after parking the car, I was thanking the Lord for all He has done for you, and for blessing your church. I looked at the church sign that said "Hope Chapel West Oʻahu," and I was suddenly overwhelmed with emotion, and I heard the Lord say to me in my heart, "The name of the church no longer matches the vision."

What?!! I was floored. My heart started beating faster, and I could not believe what Fernando just shared with me. I was nervous and a bit fearful when I heard those words come out of his mouth. I told him not to say anything to anyone about this, and he promised me that he wouldn't. We both agreed that we would just commit this to prayer. I thanked Fernando, and we both enjoyed a wonderful time at the conference!

At the end of the conference, *another very interesting thing happened.* The main conference speaker, Pastor Paul DeJong from Life Church in New Zealand, posed a very thought-provoking question to me. "Mike, why do you have the same name as so many other churches in Hawaiʻi?"

"Because that's the way it is here. And besides, the name works in Hawai`i," I answered.

"Okay…" Pastor Paul replied, but then quickly asked another question, "But what if you want to go into another town or community that already has a Hope Chapel there? Then what?"

That was a great question. There are so many Hope Chapels here on our island. I'd already tried going into a neighboring community to start a church there, but because another Hope Chapel was already planted in that town, I received pushback from the other churches. Because of that response, I grew even more gun-shy about expanding into our neighboring communities.

Pastor Paul was right. If the time ever came that we were called to expand beyond our current boundaries, the "Hope Chapel" name could prevent us from moving forward to reach more people for Jesus. And to say it plainly, I just didn't want the "drama." At that time in our church's history, it seemed to be too soon to change the name of our church. I didn't think our denomination or the state of Hawaii was ready for it, and Lisa and I certainly weren't ready yet either.

Two years passed, and during that time several others asked me similar questions. I just shrugged it off, and virtually forgot about it. Then we hired a church consultant to look at our organization from a marketing point of view. His report came back as "favorable." He loved the different elements that distinguished our church, but he also had suggestions for a few specific areas that needed improvement. *Good*, I thought. *That is exactly what we paid for. All of his recommendations sounded workable.*

Then, at the end of our consultation, he said something very interesting, "I just have one last question. ***Have you ever thought about changing your name?***"

That was it, I thought to myself! "Who talked to you? Who influenced you?" I asked. Some of my staff had inquired earlier if we would ever change our name. It must've been one of them.

Finally, he said, "The reason I ask is because when I *Google* your name and just punch in 'Hope Chapel' or 'New Hope,' your church's name doesn't even appear until page 3.

"Okay, now we've got a problem." I realized that if it took people that long to find us, that wasn't acceptable. That was the proverbial straw that broke the camel's back.

I went through all the proper channels, then set up a private meeting with Pastor Ralph Moore, and met with him at Starbucks. I brought Lisa with me for strength because I was actually a little afraid, anticipating his reaction.

I never expected Pastor Ralph's response. "Do it. Do it, Mike. Change the name! Nothing would make me prouder than to give birth to another movement. Churches plant churches and movements should give birth to new movements. Your church is going to be a movement one day." I wiped back grateful tears from my eyes.

That blessing from Pastor Ralph commenced the six-month long process toward our official name change from "Hope Chapel West O'ahu" to "Inspire Church."

I didn't want to pick a name that was trendy, but "Inspire" sure seemed to be a trendy name. Then I found out that the Greek word for "Inspire," *theopnuestos*, literally means to be *God-breathed*. Although the word, *theopnuestos*, only appears in the New Testament a total of four times, the concept is found throughout the Bible: when God spoke, breathing the world into existence; when God breathed the breath of life into Adam; when the tempest of the Holy Spirit blew through the upper room at Pentecost and filled the 120 believers gathered there with power from on high; all the way to Revelation, when God breathed life back into the two prophets who were slain by the Beast.

Even our decision to **re**name our church had been God-breathed. *Theopnuestos*! I thought it was such an appropriate name for our

171

church. *Inspire Church, God-breathed — Inspiring others to fulfill their God-given potential.*

Please understand, we were not looking for a new beginning. We weren't looking to **re**brand ourselves. But **God** wanted to do *a new thing*. God does new things, amazing things, when we head for the valleys.

> *For I am about to do **something new**.*
> *See, **I have already begun!** Do you not see it?*
> *I will make a pathway through the wilderness.*
> *I will create rivers in the dry wasteland.*
> *The wild animals in the fields will thank me,*
> *the jackals and owls, too,*
> *for giving them water in the desert.*
> *Yes, I will make rivers in the dry wasteland*
> *   **so my chosen people can be refreshed**.*
> *   **Isaiah 43:19-20 NLT**

> ***Every valley shall be raised up,***
> *   every mountain and hill made low;*
> *the rough ground shall become level,*
> *   the rugged places a plain.*
> ***And the glory of the LORD will be revealed,***
> ***and all people will see it together.***
> ***For the mouth of the LORD has spoken.***"
> *   **Isaiah 40:4-5 NIV 11**

REASSIGN

One of the best surprises we found as we hiked our way down off the plateau and into the valley was that God had prepared us for a different kind of ascent; one that we weren't quite expecting. When Lisa and I met, she was already serving in ministry. Lisa was employed by the church while working part-time behind the makeup counter at a department store. We met at a church singles event, and within fifteen months, we were married.

When Lisa and I had already been pastoring the church for eight years, we didn't realize that a major shift was about to take place. We had just completed our conference and were having lunch with two of our guest speakers. One of them was John Bevere, and the other was Ben Houston from Hillsong Church in Sydney (Ben has since gone on to Los Angeles, California to start Hillsong L.A.).

At that point in time, I had already been to two Hillsong Conferences and was radically influenced by both of these life-transforming events. Ben's parents, Pastors Brian and Bobbie Houston, had created such a challenging and soul-nurturing environment for pastors and leaders that after taking part in the rich opportunities for growth at these conferences, I was profoundly impacted, and that transformation began to reveal itself in the life of our church.

One the key friendships the Lord has brought into our lives is John and Lisa Bevere. Today, John and Lisa are very close friends of ours. This friendship, unbeknownst to me, would open the door to so many possibilities, and Lisa getting to attend her first Hillsong Colour Women's Conference was one of them. After lunch, my Lisa said to John, "I would love to have your wife Lisa speak at a women's conference for us one day." My Lisa actually said this prior to knowing that God had already planned for her to lead our women's ministry.

Lisa wasn't exactly excited about women's ministries at the time. She never envisioned herself becoming the women's pastor of our church because all of the models for ministering to women she had already experienced did not fit well with all that Lisa understood to be her call and passion.

Our background had been more conservative. At the time, we had not seen a positive example of a husband-wife senior pastor team up close. What we were accustomed to seeing in our denomination among prior generations of pastors was a model in which the husband served as the senior pastor and his wife was a stay-at-home mom. She raised the children (nothing wrong with that) and supported her husband behind the scenes. Intentional leadership was neither offered nor expected of pastor's wives. This is ironic, since our denomination was founded by a strong female senior pastor and evangelist, Aimee Semple-McPherson.

I knew God had gifted Lisa with exceptional gifts, and I also knew that we were different. Her spiritual gift mix was leadership and administration. I have never employed anyone else quite as gifted as Lisa in this specific area of church leadership. She could look at your organizational chart, your weekly schedule, the members of your team, and tell you why you were succeeding or why you weren't doing well. More importantly, Lisa never stops at diagnosis; she follows through by helping and empowering the team to become even better and more efficient at what they do.

Lisa was a part-time staff member at our church, but she wasn't considered a co-pastor at the time. She was comfortable sitting in the shadows on the weekends and pitching in when needed. We were both fine with that because our daughters were younger, and they required more attention and nurturing as young children. If you are in this season, good for you! That's such an important role that no one else can fill. But we understood that our season was about to change.

Just a year prior to my conversation with John and Ben, I was sitting by myself amongst a sea of people at the Hillsong Conference in Sydney. As planned, Lisa had gone back home to Honolulu with our daughters, and I would stay for the conference and be able to focus in on every speaker for the next two days. During one of the sessions, while one of the conference speakers was speaking, I heard the Holy Spirit say to my heart, "It's time to platform your wife."

This did not come as a big surprise to me. In fact, that gave me a stronger conviction than ever that it was time for Lisa to begin ministering more publicly in the life of our church. The big challenge was that Lisa needed to be a willing participant. She never wanted to speak or preach. She was self-conscious about her own abilities. In fact, she had been invited to speak at another women's ministry event a few years prior. In her estimation, it went so badly that she never wanted to do that again. I couldn't blame her. It's not easy getting up every weekend to preach. For some, it just comes so naturally; others really have to work at it. Even more than the opportunity to share the platform with Lisa, what really excited me was the opportunity we would have to grow together in ministry and in our walk with God.

That lunch would prove to be the beginning of the most amazing season that God was about to send us on. It would be the journey to the peak of our lives.

"Lisa, have you ever heard *my Lisa* speak before?" John asked as he folded his arms and looked intently into my Lisa's eyes. As Ben stood by, Lisa said, "No… but I heard she's great!" John sighed. "Lisa, you have to get yourself to the Hillsong Colour Women's Conference that happens in two weeks."

There was a problem. It was already sold out, and there was no way my Lisa could get into that conference on her own. On top of that, we were leaving the very next day for Argentina. (Do you remember back in the Introduction portion of this book I had shared that my lifelong dream was to go to Argentina? Well, this was *that* trip, and this was the time.)

For Lisa, the idea of leaving our daughters for a week while we were in Argentina, then turning around and getting on a plane to Sydney with only a day in-between, and then kiss her baby girl's goodbye was not going to do it for Lisa. She resisted the idea, but with Ben, John and myself all encouraging her to go to the conference, and with my strong assurance that everything was going to be fine with the girls while she was gone, she finally relented. Thankfully, Ben was able to use his inside connection to pull some strings and get Lisa into the sold-out conference.

The trip and the conference were life changing. Lisa came home after a week in Australia, but she wouldn't share much. I knew that this was my cue to give her space. About four days later, I was able to get some one-on-one time with her at a coffee shop near our home. She began to share with me about all that the Lord had spoken to her while she was away. Staying in a hotel room all by herself, journaling everything that she learned at the conference, meeting Lisa Bevere and Bobbie Houston, all of it had a combined impact on her, and a shift had happened inside of Lisa. Then she said to me, "I was afraid to tell you all that the Lord said, because I knew that once I said it, it would all begin to happen…. so now, I'm ready to tell you." And she did.

Rather than me telling you Lisa's story, I'll let her do that in her own book some day. The women's ministry that she had been so afraid to lead is now known as the Arise Women's Conference. Every year over 2,000 women gather to be equipped and empowered. They come from all over the state, the continental U.S., and even from other countries. As a man and as Lisa's husband, it is an amazing sight to see. Arise has even inspired other women already in the ministry to rise up to their full potential in Christ. Some have even started their own women's conferences, carrying forward the torch that Lisa received several years ago in Sydney. Although each of the expressions of these ministries and conferences is different, they all synchronize to do essentially the same thing: to see women thrive and to build the Kingdom of God.

Occasionally, someone will ask me if all the growth and fruitfulness surrounding Arise threatens me. I just tell them, "Of course not! It's awesome to see my wife become all God has intended her to be. My daughters, our church, and women all over our state look to her as a great role model. And I get to see all of these women and young girls, year in and year out continue to blossom. What do you think?"

REFOCUS

A while ago I was able to speak with the top-selling Kirby Vacuum Cleaner salesman in the Unites States. I obtained his name from a friend who suggested that I contact him. Now, anyone who is still selling those famous vacuum cleaners is a hero in my book because I went door to door selling a different brand of vacuum cleaner when I was 20 years old. Making the cold contacts, asking for referrals, and making the phone calls — is really hard work, and you've got to be incredibly committed. That job only lasted about a month before I got discouraged and quit. What discouraged me even more was that it was the first time in my life that I quit something as important as a job.

I also have had experience selling 5-gallon jugs of purified water. I was so intent on purchasing a Volvo four-door sedan with cash, that I picked up a part-time job while working my full-time job at American Airlines (a long time ago). I had a goal, and the goal was to stay debt-free and buy nothing on credit. So I worked for the Menehune Water Company as a salesman for about nine-months. I made cold-contacts and went door to door. It was humbling work.

Ironically, I walked the streets of the new community called Waikele when it was being built, and as soon as a new homeowner moved into their new home, I would stop by to try to sell them a contract. Back then I was selling bottles of purified water. Our largest campus of Inspire Church is now located in that same community, and every weekend I offer them *Living Water.*

When I finally made the $8,000 in commission that I needed to purchase the car, I bought my prized Volvo and resigned. That's why I have the utmost respect for people in sales.

I called that top-selling Kirby salesman because I'd heard that he used a program called "Push Month" with his sales force. During those specified 31 days every salesperson dug in deep with everything they had. They focused all of their time, energy and effort into selling these top of the line vacuum cleaners. Each and every salesperson was a highly motivated go-getter who did whatever was needed to sell vacuums after they had already worked full days at their daytime jobs.

During "Push Month," the whole team zeroed in with laser-sharp focus to work at a higher than normal pace with greater amounts of enthusiasm. During this period, this dedicated, hard-working team broke the all-time national sales records, selling 854 Kirby vacuum cleaners in the Seattle area in just 31 days!

Okay, you might not be a cold-contact door-to-door salesperson, but what would happen to your workplace, your field of interest, or your spiritual life if you **re**focused and did something similar to a Push Month?

Imagine if you **re**focused your daily eating and exercise routine. How would you feel and how do you think you would look if you ate a "clean" diet (no carbohydrates, no sugars, just lean proteins, leafy greens, a few selected fruit) and exercised with intensity for 31 minutes each day for 31 days? How would you feel and how do you think you would look?

Imagine if you refocused yourself to grow your spiritual life everyday for 31 days. What would happen if you read the Bible for 31 minutes every day and periodically prayed throughout the day for other people, for your country, for women and children suffering in oppressed countries… (added up to… you guessed it. 31 minutes!)? I know what that would do. You would feel closer to God, and you'd feel great about who you are and where He's taking you.

Imagine if you **re**focused and developed your own "Push Month" to learn a new foreign language, to study a new subject or to develop a new skill, or took an intensive coaching class online. I challenge you to employ your time in the valley to **re**focus, to get out of your usual routine, to bring greater clarity and variety to your life.

A PARTING WORD

Friend, it is no accident that you've picked up this book. If you've read this far, it means that you are serious about the next steps on your journey. If you've highlighted this book and read the Scripture passages, I hope that you'll take God's promises to heart. His promises are true. They aren't just for me or for an elite few. His promises are for you, too!

Please remember, there is nothing magical about my life. I'm just a kid from a small school in a small town on the island of Hawaii, with a lot of college credits but no degree, to date. I have been to the *School of Hard-knocks* and I've attended the *University of the Desert* (a fictional, but very real and challenging institution of higher learning in *Fascinating Stories of Forgotten Lives* by Pastor Chuck Swindoll).

There really is nothing special about me or Lisa, only that we have consistently chosen to say, "Yes" to God even when it is inconvenient at times and difficult for us. Yes, I believe the favor of the Lord is on our lives. Though I am tempted to believe that God chose to bestow His favor upon us because of our hard work I would be wrong. We love God and honor him and have decided to live a life of bold obedience. He will use that and He loves that. But the reality is that God loves us because we are his kids, and He chooses to bless us with His favor because of who He is, not because of who we are or what we have done. If you are one of God's children, then the love, blessing and favor of our Heavenly Father is available to you as well.

Lastly, I encourage you to believe the promises that God has made to all of us in His word. Take them personally. Imagine what would happen if we all believed God's promises and took Him at His Word. God is faithful to keep His promises. Imagine what would happen if we all stopped breezing through scripture passages with a comfortable familiarity and stopped to take in God's promises and *believe them by faith*. The Apostle Paul describes it this way:

"No eye has seen, no ear has heard, and no mind has imagined what God has prepared for those who love him."

1 Corinthians 2:9 NLT

This is my favorite Bible verse and the one I quote most often. I'd like to paraphrase it by saying, "Let God blow your mind!" At the end of the day, it's all for Him and about Him.

Happy Trails, Bon Voyage and Aloha! See you at the next plateau!

Love,

Mike Kai